D1118439

Kwanzaa:
A Celebration of Family, Community and Culture

Also by the Author:

Kawaida Theory: A Communitarian African Philosophy

Kawaida Theory: An Introductory Outline

Introduction to Black Studies

Essays on Struggle: Position and Analysis

Kwanzaa: Origins, Concepts and Practice

*The African American Holiday of Kwanzaa:
  A Celebration of Family, Community and Culture*

Selections From the Husia: Sacred Wisdom of Ancient Egypt

*The Book of Coming Forth By Day:
  The Ethics of the Declarations of Innocence*

Kemet and the African Worldview (co-editor)

Reconstructing Kemetic Culture (co-editor)

The Million Man March/Day of Absence Mission Statement

*The Million Man March/Day of Absence:
  A Commemorative Anthology* (co-editor)

Kwanzaa:
A Celebration of Family, Community and Culture

MAULANA KARENGA
The Creator of Kwanzaa

University of Sankore Press
Los Angeles

3/97

KWANZAA: A Celebration of Family, Community and Culture.
Copyright ©1997 by Maulana Karenga.

ISBN 0-943412-20-X   #12.95

Cover: A Kwanzaa set showing the symbols of Kwanzaa.
Interior Drawings: Chestyn Everett, M. Mera and Kweli

To my family, organization and people,

and the millions of those who have embraced Kwanzaa

in celebration and reinforcement

of the African family, community and culture.

CONTENTS

NGUZO  SABA

(The Seven Principles)

1. Umoja (Unity)
To strive for and maintain unity in the family, community, nation and race.

2. Kujichagulia (Self-Determination)
To define ourselves, name ourselves, create for ourselves and speak for ourselves.

3. Ujima (Collective Work and Responsibility)
To build and maintain our community together and make our brother's and sister's problems our problems and to solve them together.

4. Ujamaa (Cooperative Economics)
To build and maintain our own stores, shops and other businesses and to profit from them together.

5. Nia (Purpose)
To make our collective vocation the building and developing of our community in order to restore our people to their traditional greatness.

6. Kuumba (Creativity)
To do always as much as we can, in the way we can, in order to leave our community more beautiful and beneficial than we inherited it.

7. Imani (Faith)
To believe with all our heart in our people, our parents, our teachers, our leaders and the righteousness and victory of our struggle.

Maulana Karenga

PREFACE

This year marks the 30th Anniversary of Kwanzaa as a recreated holiday based on African first-fruits celebrations. Clearly within these 30 years, interest in Kwanzaa has steadily grown and so has the number of its celebrants. This phenomenal growth, which includes over 20 million celebrants throughout the world African community is engendered and sustained by the rich and varied meaning Kwanzaa has for us as a people. The holiday speaks to our constant quest to be rooted in our own culture, to speak our own special cultural truth in a multicultural world and to practice values and share a vision which reaffirms and reinforces the best of family, community and culture. As the interest in Kwanzaa continues to grow, new and enduring questions arise about its origins, values, symbols and fundamental activities. This volume is offered to answer these questions and to present Kwanzaa in the most authentic, effective and useful way as an expression of the rich and ancient legacy of African culture as well as a living tradition of great and enduring value.

I have accepted my editors suggestion that this new edition should have a brief overview of Kwanzaa at the beginning of the volume and an interview with me on Kwanzaa at the end. This is done to provide an introductory framework for readers who look for quick and accurate answers and for those who prefer an overview before engaging the longer text. The interview includes questions and answers on the origins and meaning of Kwanzaa and the challenges posed to it and its celebrants by issues of commercialism, universalism and social problem solving. The full body of the previous edition remains the core of the volume and answers questions of the origin, philosophy and practice of Kwanzaa.

In preparation of the manuscript, I have again been very ably assisted in various ways by Tiamoyo Karenga, my friend, wife and companion in love and struggle, by Chimbuko Tembo and Limbiko Tembo, my friends, readers and publishers, by Subira Kifano, my co-vice-chair of Us who also read the manuscript and offered editorial suggestions, by Adili Tangulifu, our typesetter and by all the advocates of Us whose common work, study and struggle have aided me in this and all other similar projects of any size or significance.

Maulana Karenga
The Kawaida Institute of Pan-African Studies
Los Angeles, California, 1997

Chapter 1

THE ESSENTIALS OF KWANZAA:
A Summary

The Origins

Kwanzaa is an African American holiday celebrated from 26 December thru 1 January. It is based on the agricultural celebrations of Africa called "the first-fruits" celebrations which were times of harvest, ingathering, reverence, commemoration, recommitment, and celebration. Therefore, Kwanzaa is a time for ingathering of African Americans for celebration of their heritage and their achievements, reverence for the Creator and creation, commemoration of the past, recommitment to cultural ideals and celebration of the good.

Kwanzaa was created out of the philosophy of Kawaida, which is a cultural nationalist philosophy that argues that the key challenge and crisis in Black people's life is the crisis and challenge of culture, and that what Africans must do is to discover and bring forth the best of their culture, both ancient and current, and use it as a foundation to bring into being models of human excellence and possibilities to enrich and expand our lives.

It was created in the midst of our struggles for liberation in the 1960's and was part of our organization Us' efforts to create, recreate and circulate African culture as an aid to building community, enriching Black consciousness, and reaffirming the value of cultural grounding for life and struggle.

Kwanzaa is celebrated by millions of people of African descent throughout the world African community. As a cultural holiday, it is practiced by Africans from all religious traditions, all classes, all ages and generations, and all political persuasions on the common ground of their Africanness in all its historical and current diversity and unity.

The Fundamental Activities

Kwanzaa, like other African first-fruits celebrations, is organized around five fundamental activities. And these activities are informed by ancient views and values which reaffirm and reinforce family, community and culture.

Ingathering of the People

First, Kwanzaa is a time of ingathering. Based on African first-fruits celebrations, it is a harvesting of the people; a bringing together of the most valuable fruit or product of the nation, its living human harvest, i.e., the people themselves. It is a time of ingathering for the family and of the entire community to renew and reinforce the bonds between them. Kwanzaa promotes rituals of communion, of sharing and renewal of peoplehood bonds which strengthen mutual concern and commitment. And it stresses the need to constantly seek and stand together on common ground in the midst of our differences and diversity.

Special Reverence for the Creator and Creation

Secondly, Kwanzaa is a time of special reverence for the Creator and creation. It is a time of thanksgiving for the good in life, for life itself, for love, for friendship, for parents and children, the elders and youth, man and woman, and for family, community and culture. As a harvest celebration, Kwanzaa is also a time of thanksgiving for the earth and all that is on it, humans, birds, animals, plants and all living things, water, air, land and all natural resources. At the same time it is a time for recommitment to protect and preserve the earth and relate rightfully to the environment.

Commemoration of the Past

Thirdly, Kwanzaa is a time of commemoration of the past. It is a time of honoring the moral obligation to remember and praise those on whose shoulders we stand; to raise and praise the names of those who gave their lives that we might live fuller and more meaningful ones. It is also a time to appreciate our role as "heirs and custodians of a great legacy" and to recommit ourselves to honoring it by preserving it and expanding it. We are, as African people, fathers and mothers of humanity and human civilization, sons and daughters of the Holocaust of Enslavement and authors and heirs of the reaffirmation of our Africanness and social justice tradition in the 60's. Each period leaves a legacy of challenge, struggle and achievement. We honor each by learning it and living it. And Kwanzaa is a focal point for this.

Recommitment to Our Highest Ideals

Fourthly, Kwanzaa is a time of recommitment to our highest ideals. It is a time of focusing on thought and practice of our highest cultural vision and values which in essence are ethical values -- values of the good life, truth, justice, sisterhood, brotherhood and respect for the transcendent, for the human person, for elders and for nature. It is here that the Nguzo Saba (The Seven Principles) serve as the central focus of Kwanzaa in thought and practice.

Celebration of the Good

Finally, Kwanzaa is a time for celebration of the Good, the good of life, community, culture, friendship, the bountifulness of the earth, the wonder of the universe, the elders, the young, the human person in general, our history, our struggle for liberation and ever higher levels of human life. The celebration of Kwanzaa, then, is a ceremony of bonding, thanksgiving, commemoration, recommitment, a respectful marking, an honoring, a praising, and a rejoicing.

In terms of inclusion, Kwanzaa has two basic kinds of celebrations, family-centered and community-centered, although public celebrations are also held. Family-centered celebrations may be any activities that the family chooses to introduce, reaffirm, teach and express the Nguzo Saba (The Seven Principles) in particular and African cultural values and practices in general. For example, at a chosen meal, one or more members can explain the principle for the day and say how s/he practiced it, or discuss an issue, event, or person of African history and culture, or organize an activity around the principles or other cultural focus.

Community-centered activities can be the collective African karamu (feasts) especially on 31 December, various school activities or any other collective activity which calls for ingathering of the people, reinforcing their cultural values and the bonds between them as a people, and sharing the beauty, richness and meaningfulness of African culture.

The Essential Values

Kwanzaa was created to introduce and reinforce seven basic values of African culture which contribute to building and reinforcing community among African American people as well as Africans throughout the world African community. These values are called the Nguzo Saba (in-goo'-zo sah'-bah) which in the Pan-African language of Swahili means the Seven Principles. These principles stand at the heart of the origin and meaning of Kwanzaa, for it is these values which are not only the building blocks for community but serve also as its social glue.

The Nguzo Saba, first in Swahili and then in English are:

Umoja (Unity)
To strive for and maintain unity in the family, community, nation and race.

Kujichagulia (Self-Determination)
To define ourselves, name ourselves, create for ourselves and speak for ourselves.

Ujima (Collective Work and Responsibility)
To build and maintain our community together and make our brother's and sister's problems our problems and to solve them together.

Ujamaa (Cooperative Economics)
To build and maintain our own stores, shops and other businesses and to profit from them together.

Nia (Purpose)
To make our collective vocation the building and developing of our community in order to restore our people to their traditional greatness.

Kuumba (Creativity)
To do always as much as we can, in the way we can, in order to leave our community more beautiful and beneficial than we inherited it.

Imani (Faith)
To believe with all our heart in our people, our parents, our teachers, our leaders and the righteousness and victory of our struggle.

The Symbols

Kwanzaa has seven basic symbols and two supplemental ones. Each represents values and concepts reflective of African culture and contributive to community building and reinforcement.

The basic symbols in Swahili and then in English are:

Mazao (The Crops)
Symbolic of African harvest celebrations and of the rewards of productive and collective labor.

Mkeka (The Mat)
Symbolic of our tradition and history and thus, the foundation on which we build.

Kinara (The Candle Holder)
Symbolic of our roots, our parent people -- continental Africans.

Muhindi (The Corn)
Symbolic of our children and thus our future which they embody.

Mishumaa Saba (The Seven Candles)
Symbolic of the Nguzo Saba, the Seven Principles, the matrix and minimum set of values which Black people are urged to live by in order to rescue and reconstruct their lives in their own image and according to their own needs.

Kikombe cha Umoja (The Unity Cup)
Symbolic of the foundational principle and practice of unity which makes all else possible.

Zawadi (The Gifts)
Symbolic of the labor and love of parents and the commitments made and kept by the children.

The two supplemental symbols are:

> **Bendera** (The National Flag)
> The black, red and green colors given by the Hon. Marcus Garvey as a flag for African people throughout the world. The meaning of these colors are black for the people, red for their struggle, and green for the future and hope that comes from their struggle.

Nguzo Saba Poster (Poster of The Seven Principles)
(see Principles above, pp. 5-6)

Greetings

The greetings during Kwanzaa are in Swahili. Swahili is a Pan-African language and is thus chosen to reflect African Americans' commitment to the whole of Africa and African culture rather than to a specific ethnic or national group or culture. The greetings are to reinforce awareness of and commitment to the Seven Principles. The greeting is: "Habari gani?" and the answer is each of the principles for each of the days of Kwanzaa, i.e., "Umoja", on the first day, "Kujichagulia", on the second day and so on.

Swahili Greetings During Kwanzaa

Day	Greeting	Response
December 26	Habari gani? (hah-bah'-ree gah'-nee)	**Umoja.** (oo-mo'-jah) **Habari gani?**
December 27	Habari gani? (hah-bah'-ree gah'-nee)	**Kujichagulia.** (koo-jee-chah-goo-lee'-ah) **Habari gani?**

Swahili Greetings During Kwanzaa

Day	Greeting	Response
December 28	Habari gani? (hah-bah'-ree gah'-nee)	**Ujima.** (oo-jee'-mah) **Habari gani?**
December 29	Habari gani? (hah-bah'-ree gah'-nee)	**Ujamaa.** (oo-jah-mah'ah) **Habari gani?**
December 30	Habari gani? (hah-bah'-ree gah'-nee)	**Nia.** (nee'-ah) **Habari gani?**
December 31	Habari gani? (hah-bah'-ree gah'-nee)	**Kuumba.** (koo-oom'-bah) **Habari gani?**
January 1	Habari gani? (hah-bah'-ree gah'-nee)	**Imani.** (ee-mah'-nee) **Habari gani?**

Other Swahili Greetings and Phrases During Kwanzaa

Greeting	Definition
Kwanzaa yenu iwe na heri (kwahn'-zah yay'-noo ee'-way nah hay'-ree)	May y'all's Kwanzaa be with happiness

Other Swahili Greetings and Phrases During Kwanzaa

Greeting	*Definition*
Heri za Kwanzaa (hay'ree zah kwahn'-zah)	Happy Kwanzaa
Harambee (ha-rahm-bay'-ay)	Let's all pull together
Asante sana (a-sahn'-tay sah'-nah)	Thank you very much

Swahili Pronunciation

Swahili pronunciation is extremely easy. The vowels are pronounced like those of Spanish and the consonants, with only a few exceptions, like those of English. The vowels are as follows:

a	=	*ah* as in father
e	=	*a* as in day
i	=	*ee* as in free
o	=	*o* as in go
u	=	*oo* as in too

The accent is almost always on the penultimate, i.e., next to the last, syllable except for a few words borrowed from Arabic which are not relevant here.

Gifts

Gifts are given mainly to children, but must always include a book and a heritage symbol. The book is to emphasize the African value and tradition of learning stressed since ancient Egypt, and the heritage symbol to reaffirm and reinforce the African commitment to tradition and history.

Colors and Decorations

The colors of Kwanzaa are black, red and green as noted above and can be utilized in decorations for Kwanzaa. Also decorations should include traditional African items, i.e., African baskets, cloth, patterns, art objects, harvest symbols, etc.

Chapter 2

KWANZAA: ROOTS AND BRANCHES

Introduction: Cultural Synthesis

The holiday Kwanzaa is a product of creative cultural synthesis. That is to say, it is the product of critical selection and judicious mixture on several levels. First, Kwanzaa is a synthesis of both Continental African and Diasporan (1) African cultural elements. This means that it is rooted in both the cultural values and practice of Africans on the Continent and in the U.S. with strict attention to cultural authenticity and values for a meaningful, principled and productive life.

Secondly, the Continental African components of Kwanzaa are a synthesis of various cultural values and practices from different Continental African peoples. In a word, the values and practices of Kwanzaa are selected from peoples from all parts of Africa, south and north, west and east, in a true spirit of Pan-Africanism (2).

And finally, Kwanzaa is a synthesis in the sense that it is based, in both conception and self-conscious commitment, on *tradition* and *reason*. Kawaida (3), the philosophy out of which Kwanzaa is created, teaches that all we think and do should be based on tradition and reason which are in turn rooted in practice. Tradition is our grounding, our cultural anchor and therefore, our starting point. It is also cultural authority for any claims to cultural authenticity for anything we do and think as an African people. And reason is necessary critical thought about our tradition which enables us to select, preserve and build on the best of what we have achieved and produced, in the light of our knowledge and our needs born of experience. Through reason rooted in experience or practice, then, we keep our tradition as an

African people from becoming stagnant, sterile convention or empty historical reference. Instead, our tradition becomes and remains a lived, living and constantly expanded and enriched experience.

The Continental African Roots

The First-Fruits Celebrations

The origins of Kwanzaa on the African continent are in the agricultural celebrations called "the first-fruits" celebrations and to a lesser degree the full or general harvest celebrations. It is from these first-fruits celebrations that Kwanzaa gets its name which comes from the Swahili (4) phrase *matunda ya kwanza*. Here *matunda* means "fruits" and *ya kwanza* means "first". (The extra "a" at the end of Kwanzaa has become convention as a result of a particular history) (5). The first-fruits celebrations are recorded in African history as far back as ancient Egypt and Nubia and appear in ancient and modern times in other classical African civilizations such as Ashantiland and Yorubaland. These celebrations are also found in ancient and modern times among societies as large as empires (the Zulu) or kingdoms (Swaziland) or smaller societies and groups like the Matabele, Thonga and Lovedu, all of southeastern Africa.

Of course all of these societies have their own names for the first-fruits celebrations. Among the ancient Egyptians, the festival was called "Pert-en-Min" (The Coming Forth of Min); among the Zulu, *Umkhosi*; among the Swazi, *Incwala*; among the Matabele, *Inxwala*; among the Thonga, *Luma*; among the Lovedu, *Thegula*; among the Ashanti, various names, i.e., *Afahye* or *Odwira*; and among the Yoruba, various names also depending on the region, i.e., *Eje, Oro Olofin* or *Odun Ijesu.* The Ashanti and Yoruba festivals are usually referred to as the New Yam Festival, i.e., the time of harvesting the first yams (6).

The choice of African first-fruits celebrations as the focal point and foundation of a new African American holiday was based on several considerations. First, these celebrations were prevalent throughout Africa and thus had the Pan-African character necessary to be defined as African in general as distinct from simply ethnically specific. This was important to Us given its policy of making, whenever possible, a creative and useful synthesis from various African cultural sources rather than choosing only one culture for emulation.

Secondly, the core common aspects of these festivals which were discussed above, i.e., ingathering, reverence, commemoration, recommitment and celebration were seen as very relevant to building family, community and culture. This is especially true in terms of their stress on bonding, reaffirmation, restoration, remembrance, spirituality and recommitment to ever higher levels of human life as well as celebration of the Good in general.

Thirdly, the length of the festivals was between seven and nine days for their core celebrations. In Southeastern Africa the festivals are essentially seven days. In West Africa celebrations are sometimes longer and vary from seven to nine days (7). Among the Yoruba, however, one New Yam Festival, Odun Ijesu, lasts only three days, while the Odwira festival of the Ashanti lasts "a period of one week or more" (8). The Zulu first-fruits celebration, *Umkhosi*, which played an important part in the conceptualization of Kwanzaa, is a seven-day holiday. This seven-day holiday framework was of value because it complemented and reinforced the decision to make Kwanzaa a seven-day holiday in which each day is dedicated to and representative of one of the Nguzo Saba (The Seven Principles).

Finally, the first-fruits celebrations of Southeastern Africa occurred at the end of one year and at the beginning of the next, i.e., in late December and early January (9). In fact, the Zulu first-fruits celebration, *Umkhosi*, is celebrated roughly about the same time as Kwanzaa and again is seven days. Thus, the first-fruits festivals and the time of their celebration, especially in Southeastern Africa, became a model of Kwanzaa. And the dates for its celebration were established as 26 December through 1 January.

This year-end time period became the choice for the time of celebrating Kwanzaa for several reasons. First, it would answer the concern for cultural authenticity in terms of time correspondence between Continental African celebrations and Kwanzaa. Secondly, this time of celebration of Kwanzaa fits into the existing pattern of year-end celebrations in the U.S. and thus allowed us to build on the holiday spirit and orientation already present. Not only were there Christmas and Hanukkah celebrations, there was also the New Year celebration which is an essential feature of African first-fruits celebrations. Therefore, celebrants of Kwanzaa, living in a multicultural context, remained participants in the general season of celebration of newness, remembrance and recommitment with the decided advantage of being able to celebrate in their own culturally specific way.

Moreover, this time period was chosen to establish Kwanzaa because the dates 26 December through 1 January, marked the end of the high-priced hustle and bustle of Christmas buying and selling. This allowed for avoidance of the crass commercialism usually associated with this period and for savings on any modest gifts one might want to purchase in the context of Kwanzaa gift-giving guidelines (see page 83). Finally, the time for Kwanzaa celebration was chosen to give those who wished it a culturally specific holiday to celebrate in a time of celebration. In a word, it was to give African Americans an opportunity to celebrate themselves, their culture and history rather than simply imitate the dominant culture. And placing it in the context of the general celebrations of the season offered a definite chance for a proactive choice at a time when one could clearly be made.

Ancient Values and Practices

Regardless of their differing names, African first-fruits celebrations are all focused around the harvesting of the first-fruits and have similar values and practices. And it is from a critical selection and synthesis of these common values and practices that Kwanzaa is conceived and constructed. There are at least five common set of values and practices central to African first-fruits celebrations which informed the development of Kwanzaa: 1) ingathering, 2) reverence, 3) commemoration, 4) recommitment, and 5) celebration.

Ingathering of the People

The value and practice of ingathering of the people is the first and foundational common aspect of African first-fruits celebrations which went into the development of Kwanzaa. Such an ingathering is not only of crops but also of people. It is a harvesting of the people; a bringing together of the most valuable fruit or product of the nation, its living human harvest, i.e., the people themselves. It is a kind of homecoming in the physical, communal and cultural sense. People away return; all ages, all faiths, all persons gather together in joyous celebration and practice of family, community and culture. The first-fruits celebrations are, then, a time for ingathering of the people, of renewing and strengthening the bonds between them. It promotes rituals of community, of sharing and renewal of peoplehood bonds which strengthen mutual concern and commitment. Thus, the ingathering of the crops become another occasion to pull the people together and to reaffirm and reinforce the bonds between them. This is done through collective work and responsibility (*Ujima*) for the harvest and through collective rituals which in addition to the bonding process of ingathering are reverential, commemorative, committing and celebratory.

In historical first-fruits celebrations, there was a collective emphasis on renewal and reinforcement of social relations through stress on spiritual and ethical values. This yielded a kind of spiritual healing of the people, a casting off the old and a commitment to the new, forgiving and forgetting past offenses and projecting and stressing the highest values of the community, i.e., love, brotherhood, sisterhood, truth, justice, harmony, reciprocity, peace, etc. Thus, even the soldiers (warriors) would uphold peace rather than war and stress community rather than conflict in the spirit of the celebrations. An example is the Thonga soldiers' prayer during Luma, the first-fruits celebration -- "This is the new year. May we not quarrel or kill another. May we eat and drink together peacefully. Who would have thought we would have escaped the dangers of war and drunk from this cup again? May we go about the villages in peace, not quarreling even with the stranger" (10). This, of course, is another example of the constant stress on practice in African spirituality and ethics which are always unavoidably translated in and directed toward quality human relations.

Reverence For The Creator and Creation

A profound reverence for Creator and Creation is a central focus for the ingathering of the people in African first-fruits celebrations and forms a second common aspect which contributed to the conception of Kwanzaa. It is an expression of African spirituality, which here means intense emotional and rational appreciation for the highest ideals and values of human-kind, i.e., the transcendent and ultimate. Thus, the people gather together to give thanks to the Creator for a good harvest and a good life. They give praise and pray for the good and long life of all. As Awolalu says, "The people congratulate each other and the priest prays that the year may be peaceful and successful and that the year's celebration may usher in an era of joy, prosperity and longevity" (11). Moreover, the people pray not simply for themselves but for others, for the strangers in the town, for the long life and the just rule of the king and that those present may return again next year. A beautiful prayer of reverence which reflects this is an Ashanti king's prayer at an Odwira or New Yam Festival. He says: "The edges of the year have met. I pray for the life of the people. May the nation prosper. May the children be many. May food come forth in abundance. May no illness come. May the people grow to become old men and women. And may no misfortune fall on the land" (12). Awolalu adds to this prayer emphasis on request for a just as well as long rule for the king among the Yoruba and it is the same with the Ashanti and other societies.

Kwanzaa as an agricultural and harvest celebration stresses appreciation of and care for the earth and environment. The prayers and attitudes of thanks for the good harvests and the good earth that produced them are accompanied by prayerful commitments to appreciate, protect and preserve the earth. Thus,

Kwanzaa is a time of celebration of the beauty and good of the creation; and commitment and recommitment to preserve and protect it, to cherish it and leave it as a legacy and focus of care and responsibility for the next generation. One is therefore encouraged to be profoundly appreciative of the beauty and goodness of the earth, its meaning to us and our obligations toward it and to organize and carry out activities which demonstrate this.

Inherent in African reverence for the Creator, then, is a profound respect for the creation. Therefore, a significant part of the prayers and other rituals is a constant concern to be in harmony with nature and the universe. This forms a central unit of the three-part concern to be in right relationship with the divine, the natural and the human or social. The first-fruits celebrations with their agricultural focus offered an excellent context for appreciation of nature in their thanksgiving and concern for continued fertility, natural abundance, rain, sun, plants, water and rich soil. The continuing belief is that these good things require right relationship with the Creator and the Creation (i.e., nature and humans). And rituals to renew and reinforce this rightness of relationship abound in African first-fruits festivals. In ancient Egypt, the first-fruits festival, "The Coming Forth of Min" was seen as a reaffirmation of the harmonious interrelatedness of the divine, natural and human or social (13). In this regard, the ancient Egyptian first-fruits celebration contained, as do other African first-fruits celebrations, the principle and process of restoration. Rituals were thus conducted to restore, renew, refresh, rejuvenate and reinforce the fertility of the earth, the life and strength of the people and the leader and the creative energy of the cosmos.

The principle, in ancient Egypt, of the constant restoration of the world is called in Kawaida philosophy, *serudj-ta* (restoring the world). Serudj has a wide range of meanings. Essentially, it means to raise up and restore that which is in ruins; to repair that which is damaged; to rejoin that which is severed; to replenish that which is lacking; to strengthen that which is weakened; to set right that which is wrong; and to make flourish that which is fragile and undeveloped. And in doing these things, the ancient Egyptian texts say, we should make what we restore more beautiful and beneficial than it was before. This is a core teaching of an ancient environmental ethics and reminds us especially during Kwanzaa of our obligation toward the world in our efforts to sustain right relations with the divine, natural and human.

Commemoration of the Past

A third common aspect of African first-fruits celebrations which contributed to the development of Kwanzaa is commemoration of the past, especially of the ancestors. Often this profound respect for the ancestors is called ancestor worship. But this is a misnomer, for Africans worship only God, the Creator, in his many manifestations. Thus, their profound respect for the ancestors, which admittedly has a spiritual dimension, is best called veneration. The ancestors are venerated because they are: 1) a source and symbol of lineage; 2) models of ethical life, service and social achievement to the community; and 3) because they are spiritual intercessors between humans and the Creator.

To honor the ancestors then is to honor heritage, roots, and our lineage. This focus on lineage is key for it unites the community in a solidarity of past, present and future generations. As Mends states in discussing *Akwasidae*, the Day of Remembrance of the Ancestors, among the Ashanti, the ceremony focuses on "the concept of lineage which includes the dead (ancestors), the living and the yet unborn and is directed toward achieving unity among the (people)" (14). By participating in the ceremony to honor the ancestors, the people "are infinitely reminded of the common bonds of kinship and association which make for solidarity among the people." Also, to honor the ancestors was/is to honor the best of what we are and can become in ethical living, service and social achievement. As the Yoruba teach, one is not simply an ancestor by dying but by deeds; that is to say, by living a long life of service, being righteous, and providing a model for those who come after. Thus, to honor the ancestors is to honor the blessed ones who have achieved immortality based on their good and righteous life on earth.

To commemorate the past is also to commemorate the struggles and deeds of the people, to honor the narrative of their struggle to shape their world in their own image and interest; that is to say, make it mirror their values and serve their basic and higher needs. Here, history as memory -- both sacred and secular -- is important and compelling. And one is morally compelled to remember the struggle and achievement of the ancestors. For it is they who paved the path for the living and the yet-unborn, who left the model and legacy of tradition; the tradition which grounds the people, provides cultural authority and measures the cultural authenticity of all that is thought or done. To remember, then, is to honor and preserve; to forget is to violate memory, dishonor the dead and deprive the living and the yet unborn of a rich and irreplaceable legacy. Thus, libation is performed for the ancestors, their intercession and blessings are invoked, their names are called out in a ritual of remembrance and they are given praise and thanks for their legacy and guidance (15). It would not only be disrespectful then to begin a major celebration without paying homage to the ancestors; it would also be in a real sense a serious violation of both historical memory and cultural values.

Recommitment to Cultural Ideals

A fourth common aspect of African first-fruits celebrations which is integrated into the Kwanzaa celebration is recommitment to the highest cultural ideals of the community. By this is meant recommitment to its highest and most fundamental cultural values in both *thought* and *practice*. To say culture here is to suggest a total life pattern involving the spiritual, historical, social, economic, political, creative, psychological, etc. As indicated above, the first-fruits celebrations were times of spiritual, natural, social and cosmic renewal or restoration. This restoration through communal ritual always included recommitment to the way of the Creator, the way of the ancestors, in a word, to the Good or as one said in ancient Egypt to "that which man and woman love and things that are approved by God" (16). Thus, whether it is *Maat* among the ancient Egyptians, *Papa* among the Ashanti, *Ubuhle* among the Zulu, *Cieng* among the Dinka, *Ire* among the Yoruba, it is the cultural and spiritual Good which benefits humans and satisfies the Creator. Therefore, recommitment involves a reaffirmation and rededication in *thought* and *practice* to cooperation, peace, truth, justice, righteousness, sisterhood, brotherhood, harmony, reciprocity, sharing, mutual care and confidence, the cultural integrity of the people, the Nguzo Saba (The Seven Principles - unity, self-determination, collective work and responsibility, cooperative economics, purpose, creativity and faith) and all other values which serve as *grounding* and *social glue* for the community. It is at the same time a recommitment to a higher level of life and achievement in the future.

This recommitment implied and required a process of reassessment, a solemn and serious examination of past practices and the state of things and then renewed promises for higher levels of social practice in the future. This reassessment was handled in different ways. For example among Southeastern African peoples like the Zulu and Swazi, it involved an institutionalized reassessment, even critique of leadership. This occurred within the councils of government as well as between the government and the people. Kwanzaa incorporates the idea of reassessment on both a personal and collective (family, community, nation) level and the practice of recommitment to moral and social excellence as evidenced in the *Nguzo Saba* (The Seven Principles) (17) and other African communitarian values which promote truth, justice, caring, community, and ever higher levels of human life and achievement.

Celebration of the Good

Finally, a fifth common aspect of African first-fruits celebrations which is contributive to the conception and practice of Kwanzaa is celebration of the Good. The first-fruits celebration is a celebration in the various and many senses of the words, i.e., a ritual, a ceremony, a commemoration, an observance, a respectful marking, an honoring and praising, and a rejoicing. It is thus occasioned by the solemn aspects above as well as the joyful aspects of ingathering and rejoicing through renewing acquaintances, lively dialog, narratives, poetry, dancing, singing, drumming and other music and feasting. The celebration is of Creator and creation, of life, of the people, of their history and culture, of a good harvest and the promise of the next year. In a word, it is a celebration of all that is Good in the widest sense of the word, i.e., divine, natural, social. Thus, Awolalu has summed up the festival as one of thanksgiving, jubilation and communion (18), thanks and rejoicing for life and its goodness and communion with the Creator and creation, with the ancestors and the past and among the people themselves. In this way their families, community and culture are preserved, reaffirmed and renewed. It is for this reason that first-fruits celebrations with their ingathering, reverence, commemoration, recommitment and celebration can be called a celebration of family, community and culture. And it is in the context of this understanding that Kwanzaa was given its form and content.

THE AFRICAN AMERICAN BRANCH

National and Pan-African Meaning

The roots of Kwanzaa, then, are in ancient and ongoing continental African first-fruits or first-harvest celebrations. They give Kwanzaa its model and shared values and practices, and its historical groundedness. Rooted in this ancient history and culture, Kwanzaa develops as a flourishing branch of the African cultural tree. It emerges in the context of African American life and struggle as a recreated and expanded ancient tradition. Thus, it bears special characteristics and meaning for African American people. But it is not only an African American holiday but also a Pan-African one. For it draws from the cultures of various African peoples, and is celebrated by millions of Africans throughout the world African community. Moreover, these various African peoples celebrate Kwanzaa because it speaks not only to African Americans in a special way, but also to Africans as a whole, in its stress on history, values, family, community and culture.

Kwanzaa was established in 1966 in the midst of the Black Freedom Movement and thus reflects its concern for cultural groundedness in thought and practice, and the unity and self-determination associated with this. It was conceived and established to serve several functions.

Reaffirming and Restoring Culture

First, Kwanzaa was created to reaffirm and restore our African rootedness in culture. It is, therefore, an expression of recovery and reconstruction of African culture which was being conducted in the general context of the Black Liberation Movement of the 60's and in the specific context of The Organization Us (19). In the 60's the Black Movement after 1965 was defined by its thrust to "return to the source", to go "Back to Black". It stressed the rescue and reconstruction of African history and culture, redefinition of ourselves and our culture and a restructuring of the goals and purpose of our struggle for liberation and a higher level of human life based on an Afrocentric model. This stress on restoration was evidenced in cultural practices such as renaming of oneself and one's children with African names, wearing the Natural or Afro hair style and African clothes, relearning African languages, especially Swahili, and reviving African life-cycle ceremonies such as naming, nationalization, rites of passage (Akika and Majando), wedding (Arusi) and funeral (Maziko).

This restorative thrust also involved the struggle for an establishment of Black Studies in the academy and the building of community institutions which restored and reintroduced

African culture, i.e., cultural centers, theaters, art galleries, independent schools, etc. Moreover, there was an emphasis on returning to the African continent physically, culturally and spiritually for cultural revitalization, to reestablish links and build ongoing mutually beneficial and reinforcing relationships. And finally, there was the attempt to recover and begin to live, even relive, African values in the family and community as a way to rebuild and reinforce family, community and culture.

Us, under the leadership of this writer, was and remains a vanguard organization in this process of cultural restoration. In fact, upon its founding, it declared itself dedicated to "the creation, recreation and circulation of Black culture." This, Us maintained, would be accomplished by self-conscious construction, institution-building and social struggle which shaped the culture and the people and aided in the creation of a society in which they could live and develop freely. Thus, Us argued that key to the improvement and enrichment of African American life is the rescue and reconstruction of their culture.

Us defined culture in its fullest sense as *the totality of thought and practice by which a people creates itself, celebrates, sustains and develops itself, and introduces itself to history and humanity.* Culture for Us, then, is not simply fine art, but the totality of thought and practice of a people which occurs in at least seven fundamental areas: history, religion (spirituality), social organization, economic organization, political organization, creative production (art, music, literature, dance) and ethos (the collective psychology which results from activity in the other six areas). Us further defined culture in terms of its view and value dimensions and the quality of practice that proceeds from these. It maintains that the quality of social practice is directly related to the quality of cultural vision and values. Values here are defined as categories of commitment and priorities which enhance or diminish human possibilities. In a word, what a person determines as important and puts first in his/her life determines the quality and direction of that person's life. And as it is with a person, so it is with a people.

Reinforcing the Bonds Between Us

Secondly, Kwanzaa was created to serve as a regular communal celebration to reaffirm and reinforce the bonds between us as a people. It was designed to be an ingathering to strengthen community and reaffirm common identity, purpose and direction. Kwanzaa was created to reaffirm and reinforce the bonds between us as a people in both the national and Pan-African sense. In other words, Kwanzaa as an African holiday shaped in the context of African American life and struggle was and remains strongly directed toward reinforcing the bonds between African Americans. But it, of necessity, from its inception stressed Pan-African unity also. Its stress on roots and relationship with Continental Africans and other Diasporan Africans was from its inception part of its central meaning and message. As Kwanzaa has grown and spread throughout the world African community, its general Pan-African emphasis has increased without diminishing its particular stress on African American life. On the contrary, the unity of African people as a whole is a central theme in both the values and practice of Kwanzaa.

Introducing and Reinforcing of the Nguzo Saba

Thirdly, Kwanzaa was created to introduce and reinforce the *Nguzo Saba* (the Seven Principles). These values were and are a self-conscious contribution to the general Movement call and the specific Us call and struggle for an African (African American) value system. These seven communitarian African values are: *Umoja* (Unity), *Kujichagulia* (Self-Determination), *Ujima* (Collective Work and Responsibility), *Ujamaa* (Cooperative Economics), *Nia* (Purpose), *Kuumba* (Creativity), and *Imani* (Faith) (see Chapter 3). Their communitarian character was viewed as especially important because of their collective emphasis, positive composition and their rootedness and prevalence in African culture. The Nguzo Saba were thus projected as the moral minimum set of African values that African Americans needed in order to rebuild and strengthen family, community and culture and become a self-conscious social force in the struggle to control their destiny and daily life. This stress on the Nguzo Saba was at the same time an emphasis on the importance of African communitarian values in general. And Kwanzaa was conceived as a fundamental and important way to introduce and reinforce these values and cultivate appreciation for them.

Practicing Self-Determination

And finally, Kwanzaa was created as an act of cultural self-determination, as a self-conscious statement of our cultural truth as an African people. It was an important way and expression of being African in a context in which African identity and culture had been devalued and denied. But it was and remains also an important way we as African people speak our special cultural truth in a multicultural world. The first act of a self-conscious, self-determining people, Us contended, is to redefine and reshape their world in their own image and interest. This, as stated above, is a cultural project in the full sense of the word, i.e., is a total project involving restructuring thought and practice on every level. Moreover, it is a project which requires *recovering lost models and memory, suppressed principles and practices of African culture*, and putting these in the service of African people in their struggle to free themselves and realize their highest aspirations.

Conclusion: A Cultural Choice

One of the most important and meaningful ways to see and approach Kwanzaa is as a self-conscious cultural choice. Some celebrants see Kwanzaa as an alternative to the sentiments and practices of other holidays which stress the commercial or faddists or lack an African character or aspect. But they realize this is not Kwanzaa's true function or meaning. For Kwanzaa is not a reaction or substitute for anything. In fact, it offers a clear and self-conscious option, opportunity and chance to make a proactive choice, a self-affirming and positive choice as distinct from a reactive one.

Likewise, Kwanzaa is a cultural choice as distinct from a religious one. This point is important because when the question arises as to the relation between choosing Kwanzaa or/and Christmas, this distinction is not always made. This failure to make this distinction causes confusion, for it appears to suggest one must give up one's religion to practice one's culture. Whereas this might be true in other cases, it is not so in this case. For here, one can and should make a distinction between one's specific religion and one's general culture in which that religion is practiced. On one hand, Christmas is a religious holiday for Christians, but it is also a cultural holiday for Europeans. Thus, one can accept and revere the religious message and meaning but reject its European cultural accretions of Santa Claus, reindeer, mistletoe, frantic shopping, alienated gift-giving, etc.

This point can be made by citing two of the most frequent reasons Christian celebrants of Kwanzaa give for turning to Kwanzaa. The first reason is that it provides them with cultural grounding and reaffirmation as African Americans. The other reason is that it gives them a spiritual alternative to the commercialization of Christmas and the resultant move away from its original spiritual values and message. Here it is of value to note that there is a real and important difference between spirituality as a general appreciation for and commitment to the transcendent, and religion which suggests formal structures and doctrines. Kwanzaa is not a religious holiday, but a cultural one with an inherent spiritual quality as with all major African celebrations. This inherent spiritual quality is respect for the Transcendent, the Sacred, the Good, the Right. Thus, Africans of all faiths can and do celebrate Kwanzaa, i.e., Muslims, Christians, Black Hebrews, Jews, Buddhists, Bahai and Hindus as well as those who follow the ancient traditions of Maat, Yoruba, Ashanti, Dogon, etc. For what Kwanzaa offers is not an alternative to their religion or faith but *a common ground of African culture* which they all share and cherish. It is this common ground of culture on which they all meet, find ancient and enduring meaning and by which they are thus reaffirmed and reinforced.

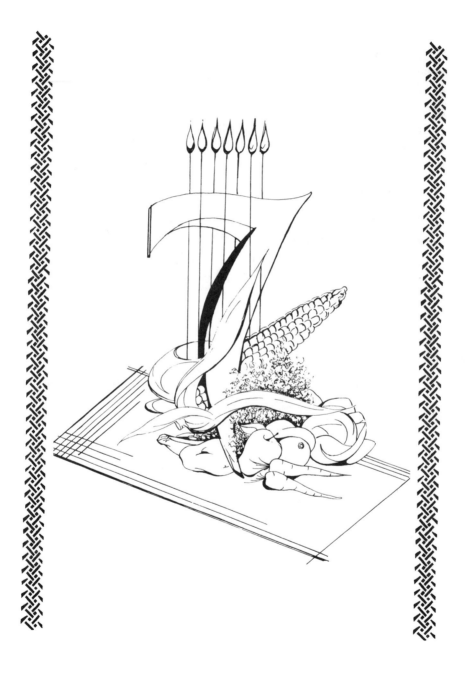

Chapter 3

THE VALUES OF KWANZAA

Introduction: Kawaida Philosophy

The Centrality of Values

There is no way to understand and appreciate the meaning and message of Kwanzaa without understanding and appreciating its profound and pervasive concern with values. In fact, Kwanzaa's reason for existence, its length of seven days, its core focus and its foundation are all rooted in its concern with values. Kwanzaa inherits this value concern and focus from Kawaida, the African philosophical framework in which it was created. *Kawaida philosophy is a communitarian African philosophy which is an ongoing synthesis of the best of African thought and practice in constant exchange with the world* (20). Kawaida is further defined by its central focus on views and values and its commitment to an ongoing dialog with African culture which involves using it as a *resource* rather than a reference. That is to say, asking it questions and seeking answers from it to fundamental concerns of human life. And no questions are more central than what values should we hold concerning ourselves, others, life and the world.

It is a fundamental Kawaida contention that values are the hinge on which human possibilities turn. That is to say, as categories of commitment and priorities, values produce and sustain thought and practice which either diminish or enhance human possibilities. In other words, what you define as important and put first in your life determines your human possibilities. The choice of buying more records than books and dancing one's life away clearly diminishes one's human possibilities. Likewise, a people's choice to allow an oppressor to educate their children have also limited their human possibilities. And a people whose paradigms of thought and practice are borrowed from its oppressor clearly have limited human possibilities. Thus, values are essential to the quality and potential of human life.

Moreover, Kawaida teaches that values are also important because they are a core component of culture and interact with practice in creating and sustaining the fabric and forward or backward motion of culture. For values support or oppose various kinds of practice which, in and through the context of the cultural process, can lead to the liberation and development of a people and its culture or their enslavement and destruction. This is not to say practice itself does not shape or give rise to values. For as mentioned above, there is a reciprocal relationship between values and practice. As Sekou Toure suggests, practice shapes values (21). But for practice to shape values, values must exist, and this, at one level, suggests the priority of values. In other words, right value-orientation precedes and makes possible the right kind of practice.

But again, it is important to see the reciprocal interaction of cultural values and cultural practice. For even though we start with cultivating the values for a particular desired life-affirming practice, it is in practice that their worth is affirmed or disproved. Moreover, practice rooted in positive life-affirming and life-developing values, creates a context which not only sustains positive traditional values, but also gives rise to new and even more expansive ones. Thus practice is indispensable but values are the original point of departure which prompts and provides guidelines for practice.

Ancient African Emphasis

The Kawaida emphasis on values, which is found in Kwanzaa, is rooted in and rises out of the value emphasis in ancient African philosophy. Whether in the classical African civilizations of ancient Egypt, Ashantiland or Yorubaland or in the smaller societies of Dogon, Dinka or Lovedu, the stress on value instruction and its inherent assumption of the teachability of the human person are evident and pervasive. In ancient Egypt, the stress on moral instruction and the teachability of the human person is especially evident in the *Sebait*, The Books of Wise Instruction (22). The emphasis is on development of character through instruction in and practice of the ethics of *Maat*. *Maat* is essentially truth, justice, and righteousness, but in the larger sense it is right order established at creation and rightness in the context of the divine, natural and social.

Moreover, *Maat* expresses itself in Seven Cardinal Virtues of truth, justice, propriety, harmony, balance, reciprocity and order. These virtues and others form the substance of instruction whose product is a good character. As Ankhsheshonqi says, "it is in the development of character that instruction succeeds." And Ptah-hotep teaches, "strive for excellence in all you do so that no fault can be found in your character. For *Maat* is great, its value lasting..." In fact so much faith is placed on value-orientation and character development that Ankhsheshonqi describes character as one's family away from home and Phebhor sees it as the means of paving the path of one's future. "If you stay in a town in which you have no people," Ankhsheshonqi teaches, "your character is your family." And Phebhor instructs, that "(excessive) pride and arrogance are the destruction of their owner but those who are gentle in character create their own fate" (23).

The concept of *Cieng* among the Dinka is similar to *Maat* and means the moral and social order given by the Creator and inherited from the ancestors (24). The thrust here also is to build character through value orientation. Education, Deng notes, is not geared toward knowledge for knowledge's sake but "aims at promoting that which makes for good human relations," and of course, builds good character which is the foundation of these relations. Deng reports that in discussing the material achievements and emphasis of the Europeans, the Dinka concede Europeans have power and are inventors but they conclude, "We are men of men," i.e., the model of men among men; or the model of humanity among humans (25). This distinction is an important one because it places greater value on virtue and character than on material achievement and possession. This emphasis and insight reminds us of W.E.B. DuBois' counter to Booker T. Washington's stress on education as essentially education for employment. DuBois' response was that if we simply teach people to make money we have only made money makers, not men and women. Work, he says, must be "inspired by the *right ideals* and guided by intelligence" (emphasis mine). Thus, "education must not simply teach work (or employment) but life" based on those ideals (26).

Communitarian Values

A second point to note about the Kawaida and thus Kwanzaa's stress on African values is their communitarian character. This African philosophical tradition of stress on communitarian values is in sharp contrast to the individualistic tradition of European philosophy. The African philosophical tradition carries within it a conception of person and community which grounds and undergirds its communitarian values. This conception contains three basic assumptions which informs Kwanzaa's commitment to communitarian values. First, in African philosophy, the true human person is never an isolated, unattached individual, but always a person-in-community. In the European view, the person is defined by the ability to think, exercise will, or possess memory. But as Menkiti states, "in the African view, it is the community which defines the person, not some isolated static quality of rationality, will or memory" (27). Thus, in defining oneself from an African communitarian point of view, one does not say as Descartes, "I think, therefore I am." On the contrary, one says as Mbiti notes, "I am because we are; and since we are, therefore I am"(28).

Secondly, the communitarian African view of personhood poses personhood as a *process of becoming* rather than a simple *state of being*. Personhood, as both Menkiti and Mbiti note, is achieved not simply by existence but by successive stages of integration or incorporation in the community. Here they stress *rites of passage* at various life-cycle points in which a person is integrated into the community. These life-cycle points of time include birth and naming, adulthood, marriage and even death in which one is inducted into the venerated ranks of the ancestors. It is important to note here that in addition to the focus on the ritual of passage itself, the struggle and challenge to grow, change and develop in the moral and social context of community is key to the process of becoming a full and realized person. As Menkiti observes, real and truly respected personhood must be achieved "after a long process of social and ritual transformation" in which a person attains the moral, intellectual and social virtues "seen as truly definitive of personhood." And in "the long process of attainment, the community plays a vital role of catalyst and prescriber of norms" (29).

Thirdly, the communitarian view of the human person in African philosophy sees the relationship between the community and person, and person and person as most definitively one of reciprocity. Reciprocity or mutual care, concern, respect is at the heart of communitarian philosophy, values, practice, and relations. Reciprocity among persons in its most noted and simplest form is "do unto others as you would have them to do unto you." But there are other forms. Ankhsheshonqi says, "do not do to a person what you dislike and thus cause others to do it to you also." Or as Khun-Anup says, "Answer not good with evil and put not one thing in the place of another." And finally he says, "Do to the doer that he or she may also do. It is thanking one for what one may do, blocking a blow before it strikes and giving an assignment to one who is skillful" (30). The most interesting and engaging form is the last form which may be called an initiatory kind of reciprocity. That is to say, it is a form of reciprocity which contributes to the enrichment and expansion of the moral community by acting in such a way to evoke a given moral response. It is not simply doing to others what you would expect, but acting in such a way you cultivate the context for the highest level of moral community and exchange, i.e., doing good to others so that they, inspired by your example, also do good.

The second aspect of reciprocity is reciprocity between community and person. This is outlined by Mbiti who poses it as a kind of symbiotic empathy and investment in each other's happiness, well-being and development. He states that "it is a deeply religious (or spiritual) transaction" in which "only in terms of other people does the individual become conscious of his own being, his own duties, his privileges and responsibilities toward himself and towards other people" (31). Moreover, the person's suffering, rejoicing, marriage, parenthood are those of the community. And the community's fortune and misfortune, strength and weakness, etc., are those of the person. In a word, "whatever happens to the individual happens to the whole group, and whatever happens to the whole group happens to the individual."

It is easy to assume in the context of European stress on the individual that such a close-knit relationship between person and community is oppressive and restrictive to the person. But on the contrary, a truly communitarian community recognizes and respects the interdependence and reciprocity of person and community. Gyekye, in discussing Akan communitarian or communalist thought, argues mutual interdependence between person and community in which each is strengthened and reinforced by the other (32). For the Akan, he notes, we are first of all social beings. Human sociality is an expression of human nature and thus community is the best context for full realization of human capacities, needs and aspirations.

Communalism in Akan thought, he tells us, is not a negation of the individual or his/her aspiration, but "a recognition of the limited character of the possibilities of the individual" alone, isolated and outside an adequate support system to aid him/her in his/her quest for well-being and self-realization. In the face of this limitation, the communitarian society seeks to enhance the individual's ability for well-being and self-realization through building on common grounds and common interests. Thus, "the communal social order is participatory (and) characterized by such social and ethical values as social well-being, solidarity, interdependence, cooperation and reciprocal obligation" (33). These values and practices for and by all create a social good which in turn benefits each person in the community.

Community Implications

Finally, the stress on communitarian values have several implications for African philosophy and social practice. First, the community, not the individual as in Europe, becomes the fundamental point of departure for understanding and organizing human community and relations. And thus, instead of giving the individual a reality outside and above the community, s/he is defined and understood in it, i.e., as person-in-community. Secondly, vulgar individualism which elevates individual interests above and against collective interests does not and cannot develop or find support. Thirdly, instead of focus on creating and sustaining a formal and alienated system of procedural rights, the communal social order evolves, advocates and practices an ethics of care and responsibility. In such a context one is not simply concerned that a procedure is fair or followed but that results reflect profound care and responsibility for the happiness, well-being and development of the members of one's community.

Fourthly, the process of becoming a full member of the community is a perpetual process of becoming, which is full of creative challenge for ever higher levels of human life. Finally, as Gyekye notes, the communitarian social order provides an "intricate web of social relationships" which not only "tend to ensure the individual's social worth," but also "affords the individual the opportunity to make a meaningful life through his or her contribution to the general welfare." And Gyekye concludes, it is a basic assumption of communitarian African philosophy that "the individual can find the highest good -- materially, morally and spiritually (psychologically) -- in relationships with others and in working for the common good"(34).

It is in the context of this philosophy that Kwanzaa places such stress on values. And it is communitarian values that Kwanzaa emphasizes as the necessary focus and foundation for a self-affirming, self-determining humanistic and Afrocentric family, community and culture.

The Nguzo Saba (The Seven Principles)

The Nguzo Saba, as stated above, are the core and consciousness of Kwanzaa. They are posed as the matrix and minimum set of values African Americans need to rescue and reconstruct their lives in their own image and interest and build and sustain an Afrocentric family, community and culture. They were selected in terms of both tradition and reason. Selected from the African communitarian tradition, the Nguzo Saba were also chosen with an appreciation for where we are now as a people and what challenges we face and must deal with successfully as a people. Our most definitive condition is that we are a community in struggle and our values should reflect and lend support to this struggle. The struggle is none other than the struggle to rescue and reconstruct our history and culture, shape them in our own image and interest, and self-consciously contribute to the forward flow of human history.

The Reasons for the Selection

Although there are many other communitarian values which could have been chosen, these seven core values, the Nguzo Saba, were selected for four basic reasons. First, they were selected because of their prevalence and recurrence in communitarian African societies, therefore reflecting a Pan-African character. Secondly, these particular values were selected because of their perceived relevance to the liberational project of African

Americans, i.e., their struggle for freedom, rebuilding community and contributing to a new history of humankind. Thirdly, the seven core principles were chosen because of the cultural and spiritual significance of seven in African culture. And finally, these seven core values were selected because of the manageability of the number seven in terms of teaching, memorization, learning and core emphasis.

The Purpose of the Principles

What was necessary, then, was to make a selective analysis of continental African cultural values and choose and establish the ones which would best serve the interests and aspirations of the African American family, community and culture. In terms of the interest and aspirations of African American people, the Nguzo Saba were developed and offered as an Afrocentric value system which would serve the following basic functions:

- Organize and enrich our relations with each other on the personal and community level;

- Establish standards, commitments and priorities that would tend to enhance our human possibilities as persons and a people;

- Aid in the recovery and reconstruction of lost historical memory and cultural legacy in the development of an Afrocentric paradigm of life and achievement;

• Serve as a contribution to a core system of communitarian ethical values for the moral guidance and instruction of the community, especially for children; and

• Contribute to an ongoing and expanding set of Afrocentric communitarian values which would aid in bringing into being a new man, woman and child who self-consciously participate in the ethical project of starting a new history of African people and humankind. With these observations in mind, we can now turn to the rich meaning and message of the Nguzo Saba themselves, both in the context of Kwanzaa and daily life.

The Principle of Umoja (Unity)

Umoja (Unity)
"To strive for and maintain unity in the family, community, nation and race."

The Essential Foundation

Unity is the first and foundational principle of the Nguzo Saba, for without it, all the other principles suffer. Unity is both a principle and practice of togetherness in all things good and of mutual benefit. It is a principled and harmonious togetherness, not simply a being together. This is why value-rootedness is so important, even indispensable. Unity as principled and harmonious togetherness is a cardinal virtue of both classical and general African societies. In ancient Egypt, harmony was a cardinal virtue of *Maat*, i.e., righteousness, rightness. In fact, one of the ways to translate *Maat* is to define it as harmony -- harmony on the natural, cosmic and social level. Likewise, *Cieng* among the Dinka, means both morality and harmonious living together. Thus in both ancient Egyptian and Dinka society, one cannot live a moral life without living in harmony with other members of the community.

If unity is in essence a principle, it is no less a practice as are all the other principles. For practice is central to African ethics and all claims to ethical living and commitment to moral principles are tested and proved or disproved in relations with others. Relations, then, are the hinge on which morality turns, the ground on which it rises or falls. In this regard, we can refer back to the discussion on character development through ethical instruction. Character development is not simply to create a good person abstracted from community, but rather a person in positive interaction, a person whose quality of relations with others is defined first of all by a *principled* and *harmonious* togetherness, i.e., a real and practiced unity.

Another way of discussing unity is to see it as active solidarity. This essentially means a firm dependable togetherness that is born, based and sustained in action. It is usually applied to groups, organizations, classes, peoples and expresses itself as building and acting together in mutual benefit. The key here is again practice. In the end practice proves everything. No matter how many books one reads on swimming, sooner or later s/he must get into the water and swim. This may be called, on this level, the priority of practice. Finally, unity means a oneness, a similarity and sameness that gives us an identity as a people, an African people. And inherent in this identity as a people is the ethical and political imperative to self-consciously unite in order to define, defend and develop our interests.

Family Unity

Unity as principle and practice begins in the family but presupposes value-orientation of each member. Adults and children must respect and approach unity as a moral principle of family and community not simply a political slogan. As principle and practice, this means principled and harmonious living with brothers and sisters, mothers and fathers -- sharing and acting in unison. It means avoidance of conflict and quick, willing and principled resolution when it occurs. It means a yielding and gentleness of exchange as taught in the *Sacred Husia* (35). The family must reject harshness and practice gentleness, stress cooperation and avoid conflict, and be very attentive to things that would divide or create differences negative to togetherness.

Especially important is the unity of the father and mother, for they are the models for the children and the foundation for the family in every sense of the word. Here the African concept of complementarity of male and female as distinct from and opposed to the concept of conflict of the genders is instructive and of value. As Anna J. Cooper, educator and social theorist, taught "there is a feminine as well as masculine side to truth (and) these are related not as inferior and superior, not as better or worse, not as weaker or stronger, but as complements -- complements in one necessary and symmetric whole" (36). The recognition of this truth and responding creatively to it is necessary, she says, to give balance to the individual and to save the nation from its extremes. It also is a shield against sexism, i.e., the social practice of using gender to establish and/or justify exploitation, oppression or unequal relations.

In African complementarity, three principles internal to it are necessary and reinforcing of both the concept and practice: 1) equality; 2) reciprocity; and 3) friendship. One starts from the assumption of human equality and cultivates social equality as its logical and necessary complement. Reciprocity among equals is morally and socially compelling. And friendship is the fruit and expected outcome of a mutually-respectful and mutually-beneficial relationship which is tested and tempered through time and is rooted in mutual investment in each other's happiness, well-being and development.

Generational Unity

Finally the family must be, as in African culture, the focal point of unity not simply of siblings and of genders, but also of generations. One of the most important expressions of family unity is the respect and collective concern and care for the elders. Respect for elders as Amadi points out is a "cardinal article of the code of behavior" of African society (37). One who does not respect his/her elders is seen as immoral and uncultured. *Elders are respected, like the ancestors they will become, for their long life of service to the community, for their achievement, for providing an ethical model and for the richness of their experience and the wisdom this had produced.* Thus, elders are seen as judges and reconcilers. It is they who hear cases of conflict and problems and offer solutions. One of the most important aspects of African respect for elders is that it makes them useful and active in the community, unlike the worst of European society which deprives them of meaningful roles and places them to the side, leaving them with only failing memories.

Also, the active participation and involvement of elders in the daily life of the family not only benefits them but the younger people. For it teaches them to understand and appreciate the process of growing old, gives them access to seasoned knowledge and experience and helps prevent the so-called generation gap so evident and advertised in European society. Key to this linking of young and old is the concept of lineage which links all the living, the departed and the yet unborn. This is translated in practice into the extended family and the protocol, ritual, reciprocity and remembrance this involves and requires. Early in life continental African children are taught to memorize and recite their family tree as far back as any ancestor is known. This keeps historical memory alive and reaffirms respect for those living and departed who contributed to their coming into being and cultural molding.

Community Unity

Now, if one starts with the family when discussing unity, the community (local and national) becomes of necessity the next level of the concern and practice of unity. The family, as it is written, is the smallest example of how the nation (or national community) works. For the relations, values and practice one has in the family are a reflection and evidence of what one will find in the community. Unity begins in the family but it extends to organizational affiliation and then the unity of organizations, i.e., African American united fronts. Malcolm X taught that community unity first depended on everyone's belonging to an organization, then all organizations uniting on the basis of common interests and aspirations. He posed community unity, in its two-level form, as morally compelling. It was for him irresponsible and self-destructive not to unite around common interests and instead glory in differences. What African Americans needed to do, he taught, is to forget their superficial organizational differences and even differences of religion and unite around their common identity as Africans, and their common interests, especially the interests of liberation (38).

Pan-African Unity

The ultimate level of unity for African people is Pan-African unity or unity of the world African community. This is also called unity of the race. Thus, when Garvey says, "Up you mighty race; you can accomplish what you will," he is talking to the world African community. The form of unity this takes is Pan-Africanism, i.e., the struggle to unite all Africans everywhere around common interests and make African cultural and political presence on the world stage both powerful and permanent. Pan-Africanism requires and urges that we see ourselves and act in history as an African people, belonging to a world community of African peoples. In this way, we self-consciously share in both the glory and burden of our history. And in that knowledge and context act to honor, preserve and expand that history in the struggle for liberation and ever higher levels of human life.

The Principle of Kujichagulia (Self-Determination)

Kujichagulia (Self-Determination)
"To define ourselves, name ourselves, create for ourselves and speak for ourselves."

The second principle of the Nguzo Saba is self-determination. This too expresses itself as both commitment and practice. It demands that we as an African people define, defend and develop ourselves instead of allowing or encouraging others to do this. It requires that we recover lost memory and once again shape our world in our own image and interest. And it is a call to recover and speak our own special cultural truth to the world and make our own unique contribution to the forward flow of human history.

Defining Identity

The first act of a free people is to shape its world in its own image and interest. And it is a statement about their conception of self and their commitment to self-determination. Kawaida, building on the teachings of Frantz Fanon, states that each person must ask him or herself three basic questions: "Who am I, am I really who I am, and am I all I ought to be?" (39). These are questions of history and culture, not simply queries or questions of personal identity. More profoundly they are questions of collective identity based and borne out in historical and cultural practice. And the essential quality of that practice must be the quality of self-determination.

To answer the question of "Who am I?" correctly, then, is to know and live one's history and practice one's culture. To answer the question of "Am I really who I am?" is to have and employ a cultural criteria of authenticity, i.e., criteria of what is real and unreal, what is appearance and essence, what is culturally-rooted and foreign. And to answer the question of "Am I all I ought to be?" is to self-consciously possess and use ethical and cultural standards which measure men, women and children in terms of the quality of their thought and practice in the context of who they are and must become, in both an African and human sense.

Afrocentric Thought and Practice

The principle of self-determination carries within it the assumption that we have both the right and responsibility to exist as a people and make our own unique contribution to the forward flow of human history. This principle shelters the assumption that as fathers and mothers of humanity and human civilization in the Nile Valley, we have no business playing the cultural children of the world. So it reminds us of the fact that African people introduced and developed some of the basic disciplines of human knowledge -- astronomy, geometry, literature, math, medicine, ethics, advanced architecture, etc. And it urges us as a people not to surrender our historical and cultural identity to fit into the culture of another. Openness to exchange is a given, but it presupposes that one has kept enough of one's culture to engage in exchange, rather than slavishly follow another's lead.

The principle and practice of self-determination expresses and supports the concept and practice of Afrocentricity. *Afrocentricity is a quality of thought and practice which is rooted in the cultural image and human interests of African people* (40). To say that a perspective or approach is in an African cultural image is to say it's rooted in an African value system and world-view, especially in the historical and cultural sense. And to say that an approach or perspective is in the human interests of African people is to say it is supportive of the just claims African people have and share with other humans, i.e., freedom from want, toil and domination, and freedom to fully realize themselves in their human and African fullness.

Afrocentricity does not seek to deny or deform others' history and humanity, but to affirm, rescue and reconstruct its own after the Holocaust of Enslavement and various other forms of oppression. Afrocentricity at its cultural best is an ongoing quest for historical and cultural anchor, a foundation on which we raise our cultural future, ground our cultural production and measure their authenticity and value. Moreover, Afrocentricity is an on-going critical reconstruction directed toward restoring lost and missing parts of our historical self-formation or development as a people. It is furthermore a self-conscious posing of the African experience, both classical and general, as an instructive and useful paradigm for human liberation and a higher level of human life. Afrocentricity, as the core and fundamental quality of our self-determination, reaffirms our right and responsibility to exist as a people, to speak our own special truth to the world and to make our own contribution to the forward flow of human history. To do the opposite is immoral; to do less is dishonorable and ultimately self-destructive.

The Principle of Ujima (Collective Work and Responsibility)

Ujima (Collective Work and Responsibility)
"To build and maintain our community together and make our brother's and sisters's problems our problems and to solve them together."

The third principle is Ujima (Collective Work and Responsibility) which is a commitment to active and informed togetherness on matters of common interest. It is also recognition and respect for the fact that without collective work and struggle, progress is impossible and liberation unthinkable. Moreover, the principle of Ujima supports the fundamental assumption that African is not just an identity, but also a destiny and duty, i.e., a responsibility. In other words, our collective identity in the long run is a collective future. Thus, there is a need and obligation for us as self-conscious and committed people to shape our future with our own minds and hands and share its hardships and benefits together.

Ujima, as principle and practice, also means that we accept the fact that we are collectively responsible for our failures and setbacks as well as our victories and achievements. And this holds true not only on the national level, but also on the level of family and organization or smaller units. Such a commitment implies and encourages a vigorous capacity for self-criticism and self-correction which is indispensable to our strength, defense and development as a people.

African Freedom is Indivisible

The principle of collective work and responsibility also points to the fact that African freedom is indivisible. It shelters the assumption that as long as any African anywhere is oppressed, exploited, enslaved or wounded in any way in her or his humanity, all African people are also. It thus, rejects the possibility or desirability of individual freedom in any unfree context. Instead, it poses the need for struggle to create a context in which all can be free. Moreover, Ujima rejects escapist and abstract humanism and supports the humanism that begins with commitment to and concern for the humans among whom we live and to whom we owe our existence, i.e., our own people. In a word, real humanism begins with accepting one's own humanity in the particular form in which it expresses itself and then initiating and sustaining exchanges with others in the context of our common humanity. It also posits that the liberation struggle to rescue and reconstruct African history and humanity is a significant contribution to overall struggle for human liberation.

Active Cooperation

In the context of a communitarian social order, cooperation is another key aspect of Ujima. It is based on the assumption
that what one does to benefit others is at the same time a benefit
to him/her. Likewise, "one who injures others in the end injures
him/herself" as the Yoruba proverb states. In the Lovedu community in South Africa, children are taught not to be aggressive or
competitive but to be cooperative and share responsibility as a
fundamental moral obligation (41). Even their language reflects
this cooperative thrust. A child in asking for something says,
"give me also," even though s/he is the only one asking. For s/he
is recognizing that s/he is not nor should s/he be the only one
being given something. On the contrary, all things of value are to
be shared as a common good. Likewise, the Lovedu's prayer is
never just for oneself but for all of their health, blessing, and
prosperity. In fact, to ask for the personal without at the same
time asking for the collective is both improper and immoral.
The lesson of the Lovedu is that harmonious living, as
with the Dinka, is of paramount importance. Thus, being
quarrelsome or contentious is one of the worst offenses. And
striving for uncoerced or free and willing agreement is the model
of behavior. Reconciliation of conflict is patient, never coercive,
and is always done keeping the person in mind. The fundamental
objective in conflict is not to mechanically apply the rule but to
reconcile the people. For they believe that "if people do not
agree, there can be no relationship" (42). And if they have to be
coerced, there cannot be genuine agreement. In such a context,
collective work and responsibility is facilitated and sustained.

The Challenge of Culture and History

Finally, collective work and responsibility can be seen in terms of the challenge of culture and history. Work, both personal and collective, is truly at the center of history and culture. It is the fundamental activity by which we create ourselves, define and develop ourselves and confirm ourselves in the process as both persons and a people. And it is the way we create culture and make history. It is for this reason, among others, that the Holocaust of Enslavement was so devastating. For not only did it destroy tens of millions of lives, which is morally monstrous in itself, but it also destroyed great cultural achievements, created technological and cultural arrest and thus eroded and limited the human possibility Africa offered the world. In fact, the effects of this Holocaust are present even today both in terms of the problems of the African continent and those of the Diaspora.

The challenge of history and culture then is through collective work and responsibility, to restore that which was damaged or destroyed and to raise up and reconstruct that which was in ruins as the ancient Egyptians taught. It is also to remember we are each cultural representatives of our people and have no right to misrepresent them or willfully do less than is demanded of us by our history and current situation as a community-in-struggle. We must accept and live the principle of shared or collective work and responsibility in all things good, right and beneficial to the community.

The Principle of Ujamaa (Cooperative Economics)

Ujamaa (Cooperative Economics)
"To build and maintain our own stores, shops and other businesses and to profit from them together."

Shared Wealth and Work

The fourth principle is Ujamaa (Cooperative Economics) and is essentially a commitment to the practice of shared social wealth and the work necessary to achieve it. It grows out of the fundamental communal concept that social wealth belongs to the masses of people who created it and that no one should have such an unequal amount of wealth that it gives him/her the capacity to impose unequal, exploitative or oppressive relations on others (43). Sharing wealth is another form of communitarian exchange, i.e., sharing and cooperating in general. But it is essential because without the principle and practice of shared wealth, the social conditions for exploitation, oppression and inequality as well as deprivation and suffering are increased.

Thus, as President Julius Nyerere of Tanzania in his discussion of Ujamaa says, Ujamaa is "based on the assumption of human equality, on the belief that it is wrong for one (person) to dominate or exploit another, and on the knowledge that every individual hopes to live in a society as a free (person) able to lead a decent life, in conditions of peace with his (her) neighbor" (44). Ujamaa, Nyerere tells us, is above all human centered -- concerned foremost with the well-being, happiness and development of the human person. And the assumption is that the conditions for such well-being, happiness and development are best achieved in a context of shared social wealth.

Moreover, President Nyerere states, that Ujamaa rejects the idea of wealth for wealth's sake as opposed to wealth for the well-being for all. And he notes that Ujamaa is "a commitment to the belief that there are more important things in life than the amassing of riches, and that if the pursuit of wealth clashes with things like human dignity and social equality, then the latter will be given priority." In the context of improving and insuring the well-being of the people, "the creation of wealth is a good thing and something we shall have to increase." But he concludes that "it will cease to be good the moment wealth ceases to serve (humans) and begins to be served by (humans)."

Economic Self-Reliance

Ujamaa also stresses self-reliance in the building, strengthening and controlling of the economics of our own community. President Nyerere has said self-reliance in Ujamaa means "first and foremost... that for our development we have to depend upon ourselves and our own resources" (45). The assumption here is that we must seize and maintain the initiative in all that is ours, and that we must harness our resources and put them to the best possible use in the service of the community. This, he says, does not mean denying all assistance from or work with others but of controlling policy and shouldering the essential responsibility for our own future.

Closely related to this concept of self-reliance and the responsibility it requires is the respect for the dignity and obligation of work. To respect work is to appreciate its value, reject its exploitation and engage in it cooperatively for the common good of the community.

Obligation of Generosity

Also, inherent in Ujamaa is the stress and obligation of generosity especially to the poor and vulnerable. In the Book of Ani, we are taught that generosity is its own reciprocal reward. "Small gifts return greater and what is replaced brings abundance" (46). And in the Book of Ptah-Hotep we are taught, "Be generous as long as you live. What goes into the storehouse should come out. For bread is made to be shared."

Moreover, Ptah-Hotep informs us, "Generosity is a memorial for those who show it, long after they have departed" (47). This, of course, is the ancient African ethic of care and responsibility which informs the concepts of generosity and shared social wealth. Such an ethic is expressed in one of its earliest forms in the Book of Coming Forth By Day which defines the righteous on one level as one who has "given bread to the hungry, water to the thirsty, clothes to the naked and a boat to those without one" (48). In fact, throughout the sacred teachings of ancient Egypt in particular and Africa in general, the ethic of care and responsibility is expressed in the concept of shared social wealth and service to the most disadvantaged. This, of course, finds its modern philosophical expression in our social thought and struggles, as a people, around and for social justice. And this struggle is not simply to be generous to the poor and vulnerable but ultimately to end their poverty and vulnerability so that they too can live a decent, undeprived and meaningful life. For only in such a context will they be able to pursue the truly human without the limitation imposed by poverty, deprivation or the debilitating struggle for just life's basic necessities. To share wealth and work, then, is to share concern, care and responsibility for a new, more human and fulfilling future.

The Principle of Nia (Purpose)

Nia (Purpose)
"To make our collective vocation the building and developing of our community in order to restore our people to their traditional greatness."

Collective Vocation

The fifth principle of the Nguzo Saba is Nia (Purpose) which is essentially a commitment to the collective vocation of building, developing and defending our national community, its culture and history in order to regain our historical initiative and greatness as a people. The assumption here is that our role in human history has been and remains a key one; that we as an African people share in the great human legacy Africa has given the world. That legacy is one of having not only been the fathers and mothers of humanity, but also the fathers and mothers of human civilization, i.e., having introduced in the Nile Valley civilizations some of the basic disciplines of human knowledge. It is this identity which gives us an overriding cultural purpose and suggests a direction. This is what we mean when we say we who are the fathers and mothers of human civilization have no business playing the cultural children of the world. The principle of Nia then makes us conscious of our purpose in light of our historical and cultural identity.

Heirs and Custodians of a Great Legacy

This again reminds us of Mary McLeod Bethune's point concerning our current status as heirs and custodians of a great civilization. She said, "We, as (African Americans) must recognize that we are the custodians as well as heirs of a great civilization." "We have," she continues, "given something to the world as a race and for this we are proud and fully conscious of our place in the total picture of (humankind's) development" (49). As noted above, Bethune is concerned that our purpose is derived from three basic facts. The first two are that we are both *heirs* and *custodians* of a great legacy. This means first that we must not simply receive the legacy as a formal historical and cultural transmission, but recognize and respect its importance. Secondly, it means that far from being simple heirs we are also custodians. And this implies an even greater obligation.

To inherit is to receive as legacy, place adequate value on and make a part of one's life. But to be a custodian of a great legacy is to guard, preserve, expand and promote it. It is to honor it by building on and expanding it and in turn, leaving it as an enriched legacy for future generations. Finally, Bethune asks us to recognize and respect our legacy in terms of where it places us in "the total picture of [humankind's] development." It is a call for us to see ourselves not as simple ghetto dwellers or newly arrived captives of the suburbs, but more definitively as a world historical people who have made and must continue to make a significant contribution to the forward flow of human history.

Generational Responsibility

Inherent in this discussion of deriving purpose from cultural and historical identity is a necessary reference to and focus on generational responsibility. Fanon has posed this responsibility in compelling terms. He says, "each generation must, out of relative obscurity, discover its mission, (and then) fulfill it or betray it" (50). The mission he suggests is always framed within the larger context of the needs, hopes and aspirations of the people. And each of us is morally and culturally obligated to participate in creating a context of maximum freedom and development of the people.

Joining Personal and Social Purpose

Finally, Nia suggests that personal and social purpose are not only non-antagonistic but complementary in the true communitarian sense of the word. In fact, it suggests that the highest form of personal purpose is, in the final analysis, social purpose, i.e., personal purpose that translates itself into a vocation and commitment which involves and benefits the community. As we have noted elsewhere, such level and quality of purpose not only benefits the collective whole, but also gives fullness and meaning to a person's life in a way individualistic and isolated pursuits cannot.

For true greatness and growth never occur in isolation and at others' expense. On the contrary, as African philosophy teaches, we are first and foremost social beings whose reality and relevance are rooted in the quality and kinds of relations we have with each other. And a cooperative communal vocation is an excellent context and encouragement for quality social relations. Thus, DuBois' stress on education for social contribution and rejection of vulgar careerism rooted in the lone and passionate pursuit of money is especially relevant. For again our purpose is not to simply create money makers, but to cultivate men and women capable of social and human exchange on a larger more meaningful scale, men and women of culture and social conscience, of vision and values which expand the human project of freedom and development rather than diminish and deform it.

The Principle of Kuumba (Creativity)

Kuumba (Creativity)
"To do always as much as we can, in the way that we can, in order to leave our community more beautiful and beneficial than we inherited it."

The sixth principle is Kuumba (Creativity) and logically follows from and is required by the principle of Nia. It is a commitment to being creative within the context of the national community vocation of restoring our people to their traditional greatness and thus leaving our community more beneficial and beautiful then we, i.e., each generation, inherited it. The principle has both a social and spiritual dimension and is deeply rooted both in social and sacred teachings of African societies.

Creative Restoration

Nowhere is this principle more clearly expressed than in the literature and culture of ancient Egypt. Creativity here is both an original act or imitation of the Creator and a restorative act, also, reflective of the Creator constantly pushing back the currents of chaos and decay and revitalizing and restoring the natural, spiritual and cosmic energy of the world. In ancient Egypt, there was a spiritual and ethical commitment and obligation to constantly renew and restore the great works, the legacy of the ancestors, and the creative energy of the leader and nation. This was considered doing *Maat*, i.e., reaffirming and restoring truth, justice and righteousness, harmony, balance, order, rightness, etc. Each pharaoh saw his or her reign, then, as one of restoration of

Maat, i.e., the reaffirmation, reestablishment and renewal of the Good, the Beautiful and the Right. This concept of restoring Maat includes the concept of *serudj ta* (restoring the world) used above in discussing the right relationships with the environment (see page 20).

Therefore, Queen Hatshepsut says of her reign, "I have restored that which was in ruins; I have raised up that which was destroyed when the Aamu were in the midst of Kemet, overthrowing that which had been made, as they ruled in ignorance of Ra (God)." And King Shabaka found a great work of the ancestors in ruins, the Memphite text on creation and he restored it "so that it was more beautiful than before" (51). This latter contention of restoring the work "so that it was more beautiful than before" is also central to the concept of restoration and was a regular claim of the king, queen, priests and leaders. These concepts of *restoration* and *progressive perfection* which are key concepts in the philosophy of Kawaida and which reflected a fundamental cultural thrust of the 1960's, informed the conception and development of Kwanzaa. And, of course, they became a goal and value of Kwanzaa in the principle and practice of Kuumba (Creativity) which again is defined as "to do always as much as we can, in the way we can, in order to leave our community more beautiful and beneficial than we inherited it." Also, *restoration* as principle and practice is central to the fifth principle of Nia whose essential thrust is "to restore our people to their traditional greatness." Thus, one has an interrelatedness and interlocking of principles and therefore a similar relationship in the practice of them.

Kwanzaa as Creative Restoration

It is of value to note here that my creation of Kwanzaa falls within the restorative conception of creativity. For when I say I created Kwanzaa, the term "created" does not imply or mean "made out of nothing," for it is clearly not the case as the above discussion on the Continental African roots of Kwanzaa shows. What one has, then, is rather a *creative restoration* in the African spirit of cultural restoration and renewal in both the ancient Egyptian and African American sense of the practice as used in the 1960's.

It is, in fact, a restoring that which was in ruins or disuse in many parts of Africa, especially among Africans in America, and attempting to make it more beautiful and beneficial than it was before as the principle of Kuumba (Creativity) requires. This, as stated above, contains the interrelated principles of *restoration* and *progressive perfection*. To restore is what we called in the 60's "to rescue and reconstruct." Progressive perfection is a Kawaida concept that assumes an ability and obligation to strive always to leave what one inherits (legacy, community, etc.) more beautiful and beneficial than it was before. It is again, in this context and spirit of the cultural project of recovering and reconstructing African first-fruits celebrations that Kwanzaa was conceived and constructed.

The stress, then, is on leaving a legacy which builds on and enriches the legacy before you. It is again stress on generational responsibility. Kwanzaa reminds us of the ancient Egyptian teaching that if we wish to live for eternity we must build for eternity, i.e., do great works or serve the community in a real, sustained and meaningful way. This reflects both a social and moral criteria for eternal life and it is interesting to note that this discussion of great works and service surfaces in a discussion by

Martin L. King on service. He said that all of us cannot build great works but we all can serve and that in itself can lead to greatness.

Finally, King Sesostris I taught that to do that which is of value is forever. A people called forth by its works do not die for their name is raised and remembered because of it. The lesson here is that creativity is central to the human spirit and human society; that it causes us to grow, restores and revitalizes us and the community and insures our life for eternity. And the Book of Kheti teaches that we should not underestimate the positive or negative, the creative or destructive effects of our thought and action. For it says, "Everyday is a donation to eternity and even one hour is a contribution to the future."

The Principle of Imani (Faith)

Imani (Faith)
"To believe with all our heart in our people, our parents, our teachers, our leaders and the righteousness and victory of our struggle."

The Foundation of Faith

The seventh principle is Faith which is essentially a profound and enduring belief in and commitment to all that is of value to us as a family, community, people and culture. Faith is put forth as the last principle as unity is put forth as the first principle for a definite reason. It is to indicate that without unity, we cannot begin our most important work, but without faith we cannot sustain it. Unity brings us together and harnesses our strength, but faith in each other and the Good, the Right, the

Beautiful inspires and sustains the coming together and the commitment to take the work to its end.

Faith in Our People

In the context of African spirituality, it begins with a belief in the Creator and in the positiveness of the creation and logically leads to a belief in the essential goodness and possibility of the human personality. For in all African spiritual traditions, from Egypt on, it is taught that we are in the image of the Creator and thus capable of ultimate righteousness and creativity through self-mastery and development in the context of positive support. Therefore, faith in ourselves is key here, faith in our capacity as humans to live righteously, self-correct, support, care for and be responsible for each other and eventually create the just and good society.

Faith in ourselves is key, Bethune taught us, saying the greatest faith is faith in the Creator but great also is faith in ourselves. "Without faith," she states, "nothing is possible; with it nothing is impossible." Also, she taught that faith in the masses of our people is central to our progress as a people. "The measure of our progress as a race is in precise relation to the depth of faith in our people held by our leaders," (52) she reminds us. As a community-in-struggle there is no substitute for belief in our people, in their capacity to take control of their destiny and daily lives and shape them in their own image and interests. This is fundamental to any future we dare design and pursue.

Faith in Our Struggle

Especially we must believe in the value and validity, the righteousness, victory and significance of our struggle for liberation and a higher level of human life. This must be tied to our belief in our capacity to assume and carry out with dignity and decisiveness the role Fanon and history has assigned us. And that role is to set in motion a new history of humankind and in alliance with other oppressed and progressive peoples pose a new paradigm of human society and human relations. As Fanon says we should not try to imitate others but rather invent, innovate, reach inside ourselves and dare "set afoot a new man and woman." The world and our people are waiting for something new, more beautiful and beneficial from us than oppression has offered us. We must, then, not imitate or be taught by our oppressors. On the contrary, we must dare struggle, free ourselves politically and culturally and raise images above the earth that reflect our capacity for human progress and greatness. This is the challenge and burden of our history which assumes and requires a solid faith.

As we of Us say prior to our doing Harambee, "faith in ourselves, in our Creator, in our mothers and fathers, our grandfathers and grandmothers, in our elders, our youth, our future, faith in all that makes us beautiful and strong, faith that through hard work, long struggle and a whole lot of love and understanding, we can again step back on the stage of human history as a free, proud and productive people." It is in this context that we can surely speak our own special cultural truth to the world and make our own unique contribution to the forward flow of human history.

Chapter 4

THE SYMBOLS OF KWANZAA

Kwanzaa, like all holidays, has its symbols. And like all symbols, Kwanzaa symbols serve as instructive and inspirational objects which represent and reinforce desirable principles, concepts and practices. Kwanzaa has seven basic symbols and two supplementary symbols. These symbols are both traditional and modern items and reflect both traditional and modern concepts which evolved out of the life and struggle of African American people.

These basic seven symbols are: 1) mazao (mah-zah'-o) the crops; 2) mkeka (m-kay'-kah) the mat; 3) kinara (kee-nah'-rah) the candle holder; 4) muhindi (moo-heen'-dee) the corn; 5) mishumaa saba (mee-shoo-mah'-ah sah'-bah) the seven candles; 6) kikombe cha umoja (kee-kom'-bay chah oo-mo'-jah) the unity cup; and 7) zawadi (zah-wah'-dee) the gifts.

The two supplementary symbols are: 1) Bendera ya Taifa (bayn-day'-rah yah tah-ee'-fah) the national flag; and 2) Nguzo Saba (in-goo'-zo sah'-bah) the Seven Principles poster or other representation.

Mazao (The Crops)

As a central symbol of Kwanzaa, the mazao represent the historical roots of the holiday itself and the rewards of collective productive labor. As was mentioned above, the concept of Kwanzaa as a first-fruit or harvest celebration has its roots in the communal agricultural celebrations of continental African peoples. These agricultural festivals were times of ingathering, reverence, commemoration, recommitment and celebration of the

Good. Thus, harvest time was a time of the "ingathering" of mazao (crops) as well as the community, and a celebrating and reinforcement of the kinship and unity among the peoples.

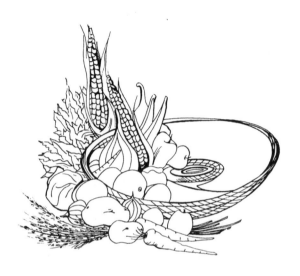

The concept and practice of ingathering is fundamental to Kwanzaa. For it stresses and creates the context for a week of self-conscious collective coming together to reinforce the bonds between us as family and community. It becomes a special time of ingathering for collective activity, communal ritual, sharing and self-celebration as a family and people.

Secondly, the mazao also represent the rewards of collective and productive labor. Inherent in the concept of produce is the idea of productive labor from which it comes into being. Mazao are produce and by definition the result of productive labor. In essence, then, they are both symbol and substance of productive labor and by extension an inspiration to its practice.

Mkeka (The Mat)

The mkeka is a symbol of tradition and by extension history. The mkeka was chosen as this symbol because it is itself a traditional African item. Since Kwanzaa seeks to inspire appreciation and practice of values which aid us in our lives and struggle, the stress on tradition and history become unavoidable. Tradition and history are foundations for correct knowledge and understanding of self, society and the world. In recognition of this fact, all other Kwanzaa symbols are placed on the mkeka and it too becomes a foundation.

The ancestors expressed clearly the relevance of tradition and history as foundation in these proverbs: "No matter how high a house is built, it must stand on something," and "If you know the beginning well, the end will not trouble you." The first proverb speaks of tradition as the necessary foundation on which all cultural structures are raised. And the second speaks of history as the framework for understanding the origin and development of a thing. A fundamental problem in human existence is to make life meaningful, to translate the flow of events into understandable and manageable terms. Events and facts alone, outside a framework of interpretation, are mute and meaningless. They assume substance and significance only when they are connected and viewed within the context of a broad and inclusive framework. History as a study and practice provides that framework, gives our lives roots and relevance and dares to answer the fundamental questions all humans raise.

Thus, to understand history is to understand ourselves, our struggle, contradictions and achievements. This, in turn, yields lessons about how we should and should not live our lives and how we can consciously take control of our destiny and daily lives. There is, then, never any total break with the past, only expansion beyond it. And this is accomplished not by destroying and denying our past, but by extracting and internalizing the best from it and using it to build a more human and fulfilling future. Without roots there is no relevance, but without growth, roots will lose their vitality and value. Continuity and change are basic aspects of the same whole.

History is thus more than roots or past phenomena. It is equally the process of becoming. For history, as roots, contains possibilities we owe to ourselves to dare, heroic examples we owe to ourselves to emulate, and a foundation of achievements we owe to ourselves to build on and surpass. Without such an appreciation for the dynamic ongoing process, promise and demands of history, reference to roots are artificial, empty and irrelevant. For in the final analysis, history is human practice, constant human struggle directed toward full liberation and ever higher levels of human life. Kwanzaa, then, is a special time to focus on the lessons and value of history.

Kinara (The Candle Holder)

The kinara is symbolic of our parent people, the continental Africans. Using a Zulu concept of the corn stalk as symbolic of Nkulunkulu, the First Born, the first ancestor and father of both our people and our principles, we extended the meaning to include our ancestors as a collective whole. The corn stalk as a symbol of the collective whole of the ancestors is used to indicate the role of the stalk in producing the corn which in turn goes on to reproduce indefinitely and innumerably, insuring the continuance of the species. The ancestors thus bring us into being, give us the legacy of life in the biological and cultural sense. And we in turn go forth to produce and reproduce in both senses also.

This concept of original stem or stalk, ancestry or genealogy is contained in the Zulu word *uhlanga* and refers to both male and female ancestors in the Zulu conception of the origin of humanity and human society. Therefore, the "stalk" or kinara is symbolic of our African parenthood, i.e., African mother- hood as well as African fatherhood. For not only is this a basic biological truth, but it represents the best of African values which recognize and respect African women for the real and impressive role in life, labor and struggle of African peoples they have played and continue to play.

The value of Kwanzaa's stress on our African origins and roots is again a reflection of its general stress on views and values which enhance and give strength and meaning to our lives and struggle as a people. Thus, Kwanzaa by putting emphasis on our African origins recognized and incorporates our historical concern with our identity as a people. By its origins and practice, Kwanzaa reinforces the fact that we are an African people who through the hazards and hassles of history find ourselves in America. As an African proverb says, "the river may dry up, but the watercourse retains its name." Thus, like Chinese, Japanese, Mexicans and/or Puerto Ricans who change residence but never lose their name or the living link this implies, so it is vital that African Americans never lose their name or deny their African origins regardless of their life and history in America.

Kwanzaa stresses recognition and appreciation of the dual historical character of our identity. In a word, the origins of the holiday, like that of the people from whom it evolved, are dual in character and consciousness. Both are African American, products of two soils and societies, participants in and heirs of two historical processes and realities. This clear and correct definition and defense of our historical personality as a people is indispensable. For identity is the key to purpose and ultimately direction. In other words, a people's self-definition is a framework for establishing a people's purpose and the direction by which it must pursue that purpose, given its socio-historical circumstances.

Africa and its people take on a new significance to us once we rediscover, rescue and reconstruct our own Africanity. The common link in our history becomes a living link in common struggle, exchange and achievement. And we realize with Garvey that the life and future of the Continent of Africa and all African people are unavoidably linked.

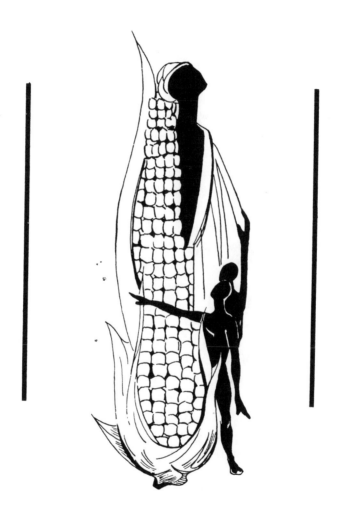

Muhindi (The Corn)

The muhindi (corn) represents children and all the hopes and challenges attached to them. Each house or family places in the Kwanzaa set as many ears of corn (masuke) as it has children (53). But each house always places at least one ear of corn (suke) in the Kwanzaa set whether there are children present or not. For in African society, parenthood is both specific and general, biological and social, and whether one is specifically responsible for a child or not, s/he has general and social responsibility for the children of the community. And Kwanzaa is a time for reaffirming and reinforcing this responsibility.

The focus on corn in the Kwanzaa set, in addition to the general use of produce and fruit, evolves from its special relevance in ancient African society as both symbol and substance. As a fundamental food staple, it was clearly central to African agriculture and life, especially in Southern Africa. Thus, it took on extra meaning in the symbolism of the community. In the agricultural and naturalistic imagery of African communal societies, the life cycle of corn represented the life cycle of nature and humans. The ears of corn represented the produce of the stalks. These ears of corn in turn reproduce themselves, becoming stalks themselves and then producing other ears of corn which reproduce themselves in an eternal cycle of life, death and rebirth. This reproductive process thus becomes symbolic of the reproductive process which insures the immortality of the community. The stalk (kinara) and the ears of corn (muhindi), then, are conceptually and functionally linked, for they symbolize the relationship between parent people and descendants, parents and children.

The Meaning of Children

Children are important within the Kwanzaa value frame-work, then, first of all because they are key to the physical survival of the community. But equally important, they are key to the cultural *survival* and *development* of the community. It is they who, as Mary M. Bethune taught, are the "heirs and custodi-ans" of our cultural legacy as a people. This dual function as *heirs* and *custodians* means that they not only inherit African culture -- its narrative and achievements, its views and values -- but must assume responsibility for its *preservation* and *expansion*.

Kwanzaa, then, places emphasis on children because they are in fact the hope and future of African people in both the biological and cultural sense. Given this reality and the need to bond the generations and develop a reciprocal respect and support between them, African communal society placed great emphasis on reinforcing the bonds between parents and children. This emphasis is present in Kwanzaa and expresses itself in the stress on parental and child affection, shared activities, and value orientation of children toward commitment and priorities that strengthen family, community and culture.

Collective Parenthood

The stress on collective parenthood is another focus of Kwanzaa. It is a fundamental Kawaida assertion and African value that children belong to the extended family and community as well as to the immediate family of mother and father. Thus, inherent in the concept of children as producers is their potential and possibilities, not only as reproducers, but also creators and self-conscious contributors to the community whose greater grasp of self, society and the world enable them to wage a higher level of struggle and in that process insure liberation of our people and a higher level of human life than former generations have known.

The task, thus, becomes one of stressing and creating a context more conducive to their growth than that of which the nuclear family is capable. Therefore, there is a need to re-establish and refine according to our new views, values and needs, the African extended family which still has retained some roots among many African Americans. The extended family is based on the African model and moves beyond biological mother and father and brothers and sisters to include other biological relatives as well as people who share one's views, values, aspirations and struggle. It provides the diversity of experiences and adult models and mentors who give African American children a degree and quality of love, care, attention and proactive and purposeful education which the nuclear family by itself cannot provide.

Therefore, in the final analysis, all children of the community or a given collectivity should not only be the *specific responsibility* of their immediate parents, but also the *general responsibility* of the community or collectivity to which they belong. This is necessary not only for the creation of a context more conducive to the children's growth and development, but also to provide, in effect, a *collective parenthood* and collective responsibility for all children.

It is in this communal context and collective responsibility that basic problems which confront the family and its members can begin to be solved with greater resources, effort and commitment.

Mishumaa Saba (The Seven Candles)

The mishumaa saba or seven candles represent The Seven Principles which are the heart and spirit of Kwanzaa (See Chapter 3). The candles are placed securely in the kinara, the symbol of ancestry, to symbolize the rootedness of the principles in the *way of the ancestors*. This again represents attention to cultural rootedness and authenticity. The lighting of the candles is a daily ritual during Kwanzaa which symbolizes both the giving of light and life to the principles themselves and the general ancient African concept of raising up light to lessen darkness in both the spiritual and intellectual sense.

To light the candles, then, is first to give light and life to the Nguzo Saba (The Seven Principles). This essentially means to bring illumination to them, i.e., make them clear, explain them, elucidate them and animate them in the symbolic and literal sense of the word illuminate. To speak their name in African culture is to make them live, as was taught in ancient Egypt. Or as the Dogon teach, speech is creative and a life-force itself, bringing into being that which is conceptualized and then communicated (54). Thus, we have the African concept of the creative word found in many African societies but especially in ancient Egypt and Dogonland.

In addition to the specific illumination of The Seven Principles in the broadest sense of the word, i.e., clarifying them and making them live, lighting the candles also has a general symbolic meaning. This second meaning evolves from the concepts of spiritual and intellectual light and darkness. Although similar symbolism is found in most cultures, it is expressed most eloquently in classical African culture in the writings of ancient Egypt. In a passage from the Book of Coming Forth By Day, there is a praise poem to truth and the bearer of truth which speaks of merging with truth (Maat) and assuming the mission of raising it up as light to drive away spiritual and intellectual darkness. It reads, "I have conquered and carried away darkness by my own strength. Truth is my body. I have come to lighten darkness and to overthrow the evil spirits therein. Those who dwell in darkness adore me. I have caused the weeping ones to stand up even though they are weary. Behold me, I am indeed the Deep one who has subdued darkness. I have driven away darkness so that light could be lifted up" (55). The candle lighting at Kwanzaa, then, can be seen not only as a general raising up and illuminating The Seven Principles, but also as a general raising up and paying homage to truth and its liberational power. In a word, it is lifting up the light that lasts, i.e., the ancient and enduring moral and spiritual principles of the ancestors.

Kikombe cha Umoja (The Unity Cup)

The kikombe, as its full name kikombe cha umoja suggests, serves two basic functions. First, it is used to pour *tambiko* or libation for the ancestors and secondly, it is drunk from as a ritual to reinforce unity in the family and community.

Libation for the Ancestors

At Kwanzaa, pouring libation for the ancestors is a very important ritual. It is an ancient African teaching found in the Book of Ani of ancient Egypt to honor one's ancestors by pouring libation. Ani says, "pour libation for your father and mother who rest in the valley of the departed. God will witness your action and accept it. Do not forget this even when you are away from home. For as you do for your parents, your children will do likewise for you" (56).

Libation, then, is poured to the ancestors for several basic reasons: 1) to remember and honor those who walked and worked before us and thus paved the path down which we now walk; 2) to reaffirm our link to and life through them; 3) to raise models before the community that instruct and inspire; 4) to express recommitment to the legacy they left by preserving and expanding it; and 5) to cultivate and sustain a cultural practice which sets a model of how our children will act towards us, i.e., remembrance and honor, reaffirmation of linkage, posing of models and recommitment. Strictly speaking, tambiko or libation for the ancestors is actually all *spiritual offerings* whether of food or drink. Thus the word tambiko may be used to indicate libation or food offering or both.

At Kwanzaa, then, pouring tambiko and making a tamshi la tambiko (libation statement) or offering a prayer or series of sacred wishes are key reinforcing gestures. This ceremony is done in remembrance and honor of the ancestors and reaffirmation of our linkage with them and recommitment to their legacy is both instructive and inspirational. It is at the same time mandatory within the framework of Kwanzaa and Kawaida values. For it is they, our foreparents, who through their love and labor and struggle laid the foundation for us, pushed our lives and history forward and gave us basic principles by which we could live our lives in strength and dignity, in brotherhood and sisterhood, in freedom and with confidence in the future.

Raising the Names of the Ancestors

Especially important is the raising up before the masses models of love and struggle, engagement and achievement in this ceremony of pouring tambiko. For such examples of struggle, achievement and social change will inspire and instruct the community to dare take their destiny and daily lives in their own hands and shape them in a more African and human image. Thus, to do "historical roll-call" of heroes, heroines and relatives is to evoke their lessons, be imbued with their spirit and be inspired to emulate their highest achievements.

To call forth the name of Harriet Tubman is to evoke the image of strength, skill and daring; to call forth Malcolm is to evoke the meaning and message of African manhood, a manhood of incisive mind and iron will; to call forth Mary Bethune is to evoke appreciation for education, institution-building, and a profound sense of history; to call forth Fannie Lou Hamer is to evoke the image of achievement against all obstacles, and immunity to breakage and compromise. To call forth DuBois is to evoke the model of the multidimensional Imhotepian (57) person; to call forth Ida B. Wells is to evoke the meaning and message of African womanhood, a womanhood of versatile mind and "won't-surrender" will and to call forth Imhotep, Nzingha, Yaa Asantewa, Samory Toure and Nat Turner is to evoke models of intellect and will, strength and struggle fundamental to the forward flow of African and human history. And to call forth grandmother and grandfather, uncle and aunt, friend and neighbor who taught us to love each other, care for the vulnerable, speak truth, do justice and walk in the way of righteousness is to evoke models of everyday, ordinary people who taught us to be the best of what it means to be African by teaching us ancient and enduring African values. Thus historical roll-call of both the great and the good, the general ancestor and the specific relative, *those who achieved* and *those who served* are equally important in offering models of human accomplishment and possibility. And Kwanzaa is a special time for such an invocation and homage.

Zawadi (The Gifts)

The zawadi are symbolic of the seeds sown by the children, i.e., commitments made and kept, and of the fruits of the labor of the parents. Traditionally, gifts were given of what was made or grown. Thus, it was an act of sharing and a labor of love and tended to avoid the alienated gift-giving which involves purchasing to impress rather than to please and share. During the first Kwanzaa in 1966, advocates of Us argued the pro's and con's of gift-giving around the questions of whether it would duplicate the negatives of Christmas gift-giving. Out of those discussions came the following principles and practice which we developed as preventives to the problems which often accompany Christmas gift-giving.

Guidelines for Gift-giving

First, we decided that even though we respected the desire of our children to have gifts at that time because of peer concerns and the relentless push of seasonal advertising, Kwanzaa gift-giving would not be automatic or done without reference to the needs of the people and their struggle. Kwanzaa gift-giving by the internal demands of the holiday had to be designed to be instructive and inspirational. Kwanzaa gift giving was, therefore, established first to encourage further in our children the making and keeping of commitments of personal growth and achievement which benefit the collective. Our intention was to establish and reinforce the concept that practical and emotional commitments to a principled and productive life is rewarded, not only in terms of receiving gifts, but also in terms of internal growth and satisfaction as well as benefit to the community. Thus, such a practice, we felt could, if handled correctly, serve as positive reinforcement for the of social achievement and progressive perfection which would benefit not only the child and immediate family, but also our people.

Secondly, we decided that Kwanzaa gift-giving had to be open and informed so that parents would receive due credit for their sacrifice and hard work to provide their children with the gifts. This, in fact, also put an end to the negative and demeaning practice of reducing African American parents to the role of mediators and messengers for a European cultural symbol in red and white, promising things that he could not deliver and had no idea of whether the parents could either. Such an arrangement not only makes a mockery of reality, but also damages the image of loving and productive parents in the process.

Thirdly, it was agreed that in order to escape the economic entrapment of Christmas advertising, we would not buy presents until after Christmas and also observe some basic guidelines. These include the stipulations that: 1) children be the main recipient of Kwanzaa gifts; 2) that the gifts be given on the basis of commitments made and kept; and 3) that they not be mandatory or excessive. To purchase gifts after Christmas is to take advantage of after-Christmas sales and thus escape the exorbitant prices established for the season. Secondly, making children the main recipients of gifts rightly lowers the number of recipients and in many cases also lowers the price of the gifts. Thirdly, to make the gift equal in value to the achievement record moderates the mania for unrestricted buying just for the season or in response to the open or subliminal seduction of advertisers. And fourthly, the stipulation that the gifts not be mandatory or excessive relieves poor parents of feeling that they have to compete with the Jones and Jenkins or even the Omowales, regardless of the economic burdens this imposes on them.

The final condition agreed upon to save Kwanzaa gift-giving from the negatives of Christmas gift-giving was the stipulation that it never be alienated either in terms of the practice or the purpose. This essentially means two things. First, it means that gifts will never be given as a substitute for parental love, attention and involvement with the child on every level of her/his life. Kwanzaa, seeks to establish and reinforce warm, meaningful and authentic exchanges between parents and children and to counter the alienated and alienating practices of giving expensive gifts in substitute for ourselves. Thus, Kwanzaa gift-giving revolves around and respects the fact that the gift is but an extension of ourselves and includes a vital part of us, i.e., our love and concern which the gift should express or it is meaningless - or worse, a mockery.

Secondly, in order to avoid lack or poverty of purpose in our gift-giving, we agreed that Kwanzaa gifts must always include two items: a) a book, and b) a heritage symbol - regardless of what else is given. This stipulation clearly points to our priorities of building and liberating our people. The book reflects and reinforces our commitment to education as an indispensable part of the struggle for liberation and reconstruction. It fits firmly in the framework of the Kawaida contention that a key struggle is to recover and reconstruct our culture and history and begin to reshape reality in our own image and according to our own needs. The heritage symbol can be an African art object; a *talasimu* (58); a picture of Fannie Lou Hamer, Malcolm X, Mary M. Bethune, Martin L. King, W.E.B. DuBois, Anna J. Cooper, or any other hero or heroine; or any appropriate representation of our history and culture. Its purpose is to keep us constantly in touch with ourselves, our history and our own humanity. In a word, it is to shield us from the vulgar envelopment by the views and of the dominant society, remind us of the richness of our past and point to the unlimited possibilities of our future.

Bendera (The National Flag)

The bendera is the Black, Red and Green national flag given to us by the Hon. Marcus Garvey. Garvey, upon establishing the colors, ordered them as Red, Black and Green, explaining that Red was for the blood of our people not shed in vain; Black was for the faces of our people and Green was for our hope. In the 60's we reordered the colors and slightly adjusted their interpretation to correspond to our current needs. Thus, we said the colors are Black, Red and Green. Black for the people; Red for our continuing struggle and Green for the future we shall build out of struggle.

We put Black first because, in fact, the people come first, then Red for the struggle which is carried by and for the people and finally Green which is the future for the people which comes our of their struggle. The stress and focus here then is on the people. They are the priority and thus are placed first. This not only gives them the priority focus and stress they deserve but demonstrates a logic of process, i.e., first the people, then the struggle, then the future shaped and insured by struggle. The message here is that without the people, nothing; and that only with the struggle can a future of choice and fulfillment be a-chieved.

Red was interpreted as struggle rather then simply "our blood not shed in vain" to give it a more broad and proactive meaning. Not only does this allow then for all forms of struggle for a free and fulfilling life, but it also focuses on the struggle as a necessary process for each person and the people in order to achieve any and everything of value, i.e., a real and meaningful future. None of these changes was made to dismiss or dishonor the legacy of Garvey but rather to honor it by building on and expanding it. Its core meaning and value must and do remain.

Again, we see that the struggle is central and multi-dimensional as our history has shown. Not only is it physical and political, it is also mental, educational, an effort to break the historical monopoly the oppressor has had on our minds and begin to redefine and reshape the world in our own image and interests. Thus, education and demonstration, confrontation and negotiation, armed and non-violent resistance has marked our struggle. Therefore the call for study is a part and prerequisite for a successful struggle for liberation and reconstruction of our lives and history. Likewise, the struggle to overturn ourselves and live a new Afrocentric life is as central as our confrontation with those who oppress us.

Finally, Green is for the future which is shaped and insured by our struggle to control and shape our destiny and daily lives. It is a future for which we must plan and work diligently. As the Book of Kheti says, "It is good to work for the future. And everyday is a donation to eternity and even one hour is a contribution to the future." (59) In other words, to rely on chance is to risk failure, but to plan and work for the future is to shape it in your own image and interests. The bendera colors, then, picture African American people in motion, studying, defending and developing themselves and daring to build the basis for a new world and new men and women to live and love freely in it, shaping it in their own image and according to their own needs, and then contributing with other peoples to the forward flow of human history. It is this image and lesson of a people in self-conscious motion for the future then that becomes a central focus and stress of Kwanzaa.

The Nguzo Saba Poster (Poster of The Seven Principles)

The Nguzo Saba poster or some form of the written Nguzo Saba should always be a part of the Kwanzaa set. For it is these seven principles which give Kwanzaa its core and seven days of cultural focus.

Chapter 5
_____

THE ACTIVITIES OF KWANZAA

Pouring Tambiko (Libation)

There are several Kwanzaa activities which should be explained procedurally. The first is pouring the tambiko or libation for the ancestors. Its significance has already been explained in the section on the kikombe (see page 80) and thus, need not be explained again here. However, it would be of benefit if procedures for its performance were explained.

Performing tambiko requires a kikombe or cup which is filled with juice or water, depending on collective preference, and held with one or both hands by the person performing the tambiko, and a large bowl filled with green leafy vegetables. The tradition, however, has been that either a priest or an mzee (elder) performs it -- the first because of his/her knowledge, commitment and avowed function and the latter because of his/her long-term contribution to the national community. It is optional, in the final analysis, depending on collective desire and decision.

As tambiko is poured, a tamshi la tambiko (libation statement) is made. One may also say words before and after the pouring of the libation. The libation statement is made honoring, praising and committing our people to the historic tasks begun by our ancestors. What is said is optional, but it should fall within the framework of praise and commitment. A standard tamshi follows:

TAMSHI LA TAMBIKO
(The Libation Statement)

Our fathers and mothers came here, lived, loved, struggled and built here. At this place, their love and labor rose like the sun and gave strength and meaning to the day. For them, then, who gave so much we give in return. On this same soil we will sow our seeds, and build and move in unity and strength. Here, too, we will continue their struggle for liberation and a higher level of human life. May our eyes be the eagle, our strength be the elephant, and the boldness of our life be like the lion. And may we remember and honor our ancestors and the legacy they left for as long as the sun shines and the waters flow.

For our people everywhere then:

For Shaka, Samory, and Nzingha and all the others known and unknown who defended our ancestral land, history and humanity from alien invaders;

For Garvey, Muhammad, Malcolm, and King; Harriet, Fannie Lou, Sojourner, Bethune, and Nat Turner and all the others who dared to define, defend, and develop our interests as a people;

For our children and the fuller and freer lives they will live because we struggle;

For Kawaida and the Nguzo Saba, the new system of views and values which gives identity, purpose, and direction to our lives;

For the new world we struggle to build;

And for the continuing struggle through which we will inevitably rescue and reconstruct our history and humanity in our own image and according to our own needs.

After the tambiko is poured into the bowl, the performer of the tambiko drinks from the kikombe and leads the Harambee (a call to unity and collective work and struggle) in which everyone participates. Although the usual Harambee is carried out with raised hands and a downward pull, these tambiko Harambee are traditionally done just verbally though vigorously. After the collective Harambee, the kikombe is passed around, first to the wazee (elders) in respect and then to others in turn. In small and intimate groups, everyone drinks from the same cup, but in much larger groups as a matter of facility and sanitary concerns, only the performer drinks from the cup as a symbolic gesture for all. Any other arrangements may be agreed upon collectively.

Raising the Names of the Ancestors

Moreover, at community or family celebrations of Kwanzaa, the historic or ancestral roll-call, i.e., calling out or raising the names of ancestral heroes, heroines and departed relatives is a meaningful and spiritually uplifting ritual. The person in charge or Master/Mistress of Ceremony can simply offer an opportunity in the program for raising the names and bearing witness to those whose lives give instruction and inspiration to the national community and/or one's family. Thus people throughout the audience stand and call out the name of a relative or hero or heroine and optionally say a sentence or two about them. Again, this is a strongly reinforcing and inspirational activity.

The Harambee

Another activity and reinforcing gesture is the Harambee which as explained above is a call to unity and collective work and struggle. We of the Organization Us took the call itself from a practice in East Africa in 1965 and added to the verbal call the raising of the right arm with open hand and pulling down and closing our hand into a fist at the same time. This was done for two reasons. First, it was to simulate the raised power fist which was at the time a basic Black Power symbol. Secondly, it was done because the word "Harambee" was a chant continental Africans used when pulling and thus, its general meaning is "let's all pull together." Also, Harambee are usually done in sets of seven in honor and reinforcement of the Nguzo Saba, and may be done at anytime to urge unity and collective work and struggle.

Lighting of the Mishumaa (Candles)

As explained above, the lighting of the candles is in honor and reinforcement of our commitment to the Nguzo Saba, the core values of Kawaida. Any member may light the candles, but it is important that children do this where possible. This not only gives them a central role in the Kwanzaa celebration, but it also gives them the responsibility of learning and being able to explain the Nguzo Saba. This in turn reinforces their respect and absorption of these values which are vital to their growth and development.

The number of candles used as explained above are seven and include one black, three red and three green candles. The black candle is placed in front and in the center of the kinara, the three red candles are placed on the left, and the three green candles are placed on the right of the kinara. Each day a candle is lit to symbolize one of the Nguzo Saba. After it is lit, it is explained by the person lighting it and used as the main topic of discussion for that day.

The black candle is the center candle because it represents Black people in unity, and unity is the central or foundational principle. Also, the black candle is the first candle lit, because it is the First Principle of the Nguzo Saba. Beginning with the second day, the candles are lit on the left and the right alternately. This is done because the candles on the left are red and represent struggle which comes before a fruitful (green) future can be assured. Thus, the practice of lighting the red then the green candle is a statement and reinforcement of the fact that there can be no future unless and until there is struggle. Finally, each candle which has been lit, is relit along with the candles of the day until the last candle has been lit on the last day of Kwanzaa.

Kwanzaa Greetings

Usually, we greet in Swahili by saying, "Habari gani?" or "what news?" and the answer is "njema" or "good news." However, during the week of Kwanzaa, the answer is not "njema," but the name of each day, i.e., "Umoja," "Kujichagulia,"

"Ujima," etc. Therefore, on the first day, the greeting would be "Habari gani?" and the reply, "Umoja;" and on the second day the greeting would be "Habari gani?" and the answer would be "Kujichagulia" and so on.

A second greeting is the phrase for "Happy Kwanzaa" which is "Kwanzaa yenu iwe na heri" and literally translated is "May y'all's Kwanzaa be with happiness." We say "y'all" rather than "you", because it is a traditional value to always speak in the collective even when speaking to or greeting one person. For communal values mean that a person is always part of a greater collectivity and thus, is never alone or speaking just for her/himself.

It is important to avoid the tendency among non-Swahili speaking African Americans to simply look in a Swahili dictionary, put words together in an English manner, and say them without regard to rules of Swahili grammar. For example, many people say "Furaha Kwanzaa" which literally means "Happiness Kwanzaa." This sounds like saying "Happiness Christmas" for "Happy Christmas." The need is to check with a bonafide Swahili speaker and avoid taking unnecessary latitude with the language.

One last note, traditionally we shortened the phrase "Kwanzaa yenu iwe na heri" to just simply saying "heri." For it is a holiday season and saying "heri" means happiness, blessedness, good luck, success, and just about anything else good. Also, it is important to note that "heri" is not pronounced "hurry," as it might seem to English speakers who do not roll "r's"; it is pronounced more like "heady" with an unemphasized "d" for those who have problems rolling "r's."

The Day of Meditation (Siku ya Taamuli)

The last day of Kwanzaa is the first day of the new year, January 1. Historically this has been for African people a time of sober assessment of things done and things to do, of self-reflection and reflection on the life and future of the people and of recommitment to their highest cultural values in a special way. Following in this tradition, it is for us then a time to ask and answer soberly and humbly the three Kawaida questions: Who am I; am I really who I say I am; and am I all I ought to be? And it is, of necessity, a time to recommit ourselves to our highest ideals, in a word, to the best of what it means to be both African and human in the fullest sense. This *Day of Assessment* or *Day of Meditation* is noted in the first-fruits celebration of the Akan by J.B. Danquah. He states that the Akan have one day during the first-fruits harvest in which they simply engage in quiet reflection. "The idea on this (day) is to maintain a quiet, humble and calm attitude with regard to oneself and towards one's neighbors" (60). It is thus a good time for reassessment and recommitment on a personal and family level.

Closely related to this is an activity also noted by both Danquah and Sarpong, the *Day of Remembrance* of the ancestors or the Adae celebration. We referred to it above as Akwasidae, but one could also use one of the days of Kwanzaa to pay special homage to the ancestors--those of the national community and those of the family. And this Day of Remembrance may also be a part of the Day of Meditation or more precisely, The Day of Assessment.

Umoja Night and the Candle Lighting Ceremony

Umoja Night and the candle lighting ceremony by community leaders is another central activity of Kwanzaa. This is rooted in the Zulu's and others' practice of dividing the first-fruits festival into two parts. These are called in Zulu the *Umkhosi Omncane* and *Umkhosi Omkhulu*. The first is the Little Festival and the second is the Great Festival. The Little Festival is for leaders of the national community to reinforce the bonds between them and to plan and discuss issues of national importance. The Great Festival is for the masses and is for mass and leadership interaction. The Organization Us uses Umoja Night to bring the leaders of the community together and reinforce the bonds between them. Each person lights a candle and offers a wish within the framework of one of The Seven Principles for the community.

The Karamu (Feast)

The Karamu (Feast) is also a central activity of Kwanzaa. The night of the Karamu on December 31 had traditionally been for adults, but children can participate if the activities are scheduled early enough. Another alternative is that they have their own Karamu at home, at school, at a cultural center or at their organizational headquarters. For Kwanzaa Karamu are exciting and enjoyable events and children should be able to participate in them in some meaningful manner whether with adults or among themselves.

The night of the Kwanzaa Karamu is a very special occasion because it is a community and cooperative project of ceremonies, tambiko, cultural expressions and a magnificent feast of various foods prepared by all attending. Traditionally, the food for the night is contributed by each participating house (family) which prepares an agreed upon dish or dishes. This agreement is to avoid unnecessary foods and to increase the variety. Therefore, there is always an abundance of food, especially in consideration of a person who may not be economically capable of providing food. However, usually everyone, even single persons, can bring fruit, bread or other similar items, so that everyone can contribute to the collective project (Ujima) and through that be and feel a vital part of the collective exchange and enjoyment. Although the food is traditionally brought by participants, community catering for increasingly large celebrations has become customary also.

The place where the Karamu takes place is also decorated like our homes, in an African motif using a black, red and green color scheme. A large Kwanzaa setting is also placed in the room of the Karamu, and a large mkeka is placed in the center of the floor where all the food is placed creatively and made easily accessible to all for self-service. Before and during the feast, an informative and entertaining program is presented. Traditionally, the program involved welcoming, remembering, reassessment, recommitment and rejoicing, concluded by a farewell statement and call for greater unity and struggle.

Tamshi La Tutaonana (Farewell Statement)

A final reinforcing gesture is the tamshi la tutaonana and Harambee. The farewell statement is used to close out the karamu and, in fact, end the year. It, like other Kwanzaa activities and procedures, contains praise of our value system and is a call for commitment to it and ourselves. It ends with the community standing and being led in the Harambee by the person who makes the tamshi. The Tamshi la Tutaonana we traditionally use and which can serve as a model for others is, in both spirit and content, an excellent way to end our celebration (see below).

Decorating For Kwanzaa

It is good to begin checking the first week in December to see what symbols and other items you have and don't have for Kwanzaa. The advantage of this is that it allows two weeks for preparation before decorations are put up which is a week before Kwanzaa. If you do not have a particular symbol or other item, you then will have ample time to make it or find and buy it. Some items are better made than bought however. In this regard, the kinara easily comes to mind. For example, some persons tend to want to avoid any inconvenience of finding African shops and will lean toward buying from anyone or buying a Jewish menorah as a substitute for the kinara. This causes at least four problems.

First, it invites unnecessary and strained comparisons between the kinara and the menorah. Secondly, it represents a culturally and aesthetically incompatible insertion in the context of an African motif. Thirdly, it represents a non-creative gesture and thus, is a violation of both the Second and Sixth Principles, i.e., Kujichagulia and Kuumba. The problems, however, can be solved with one bold stroke of Kuumba, a piece of aesthetic driftwood (or any other kind of wood beautifully constructed or carved) and some screw-in candle holders. Also, vinara (candle holders) are easily obtained now from African shops that sell Kwanzaa items. But in any case high standards are imperative.

Another negative tendency is to use a cornucopia to hold the mazao. This also is culturally and aesthetically incompatible with an African motif. An inexpensive yet tasteful basket from

Africa, a modified one from the U.S. or none at all would serve the purpose and keep the spirit and principle on firm cultural ground. Again though, high standards of beauty and creativity are imperative. Making one's own cards at home, or buying them from an African store is optional. But the standing rule is that the closer we stay to creativity the better. Everything used for Kwanzaa does not have to be made at home but it is obvious such creative activity reinforces the principles and purpose of Kwanzaa.

Keep in mind that decor must be in an African motif and that black, red and green should be prominent colors in it. Begin assembling things needed that are inexpensive and available, but without violating standards. Crepe paper, plants, fruits and vegetables, pictures of African people and scenery are such useable items. To begin decorating, first choose a low table for the Kwanzaa setting, i.e., the Kwanzaa symbols. Usually, the table is covered with a piece of African material, and on that, the mkeka is placed. Beginning with the kinara, the other Kwanzaa symbols are then placed on top of the mkeka. The mishumaa saba (seven candles) which include one black, three red and three green should be arranged, as explained above, so that the black is in front or center of the kinara, the three red on the left and the three green on the right.

The muhindi or masuke (ears of corn) are placed in numbers that correspond to the number of children in the family. But even if the family has none, at least one suke (ear of corn) is still placed in the mkeka to symbolize the potential for children as well as the African concept of social parenthood, i.e., all the children of the community are ours collectively. The remaining Kwanzaa symbols, the mazao (crops), kikombe cha umoja (unity cup) and the zawadi (gifts) are also aesthetically arranged on top of the mkeka. The zawadi (gifts) of books and the heritage symbol may be placed aesthetically around the Kwanzaa setting. The other zawadi, are placed to the side, never dominating the Kwanzaa setting. Then plants and other decorative items may be placed, according to eye and taste next to the Kwanzaa setting. Also, a copy of the Nguzo Saba may be placed on the wall directly above the Kwanzaa setting to remind us everyday of each principle and inspire us to work harder to practice these principles. Crepe paper, streamers and other items may be used to decorate the entire house and the bendera may be placed behind the Nguzo Saba, so that the colors also are powerfully projected to stress their significance. These are just a few suggestions which are basics. The rest is and should be left to the tastes and creative abilities and interests of members of each house which are expressed within the general framework of an African motif. *In conclusion, be sure to be careful in using only that which affirms the dignity of the celebration and the culture and speaks to the rich beauty and profound meaning of both.*

Basic Activities

Each day of Kwanzaa, as mentioned above, the family sits down at meals or other times and discusses the particular principle for that day. For example, on Umoja Night the family discusses the principle of Umoja (Unity). Then the Umoja candle is lit by the person who volunteers to discuss that principle for that day in terms of its meaning and importance. Naturally the principles should be discussed in such a way that children receive practical day-to-day examples in order to facilitate their understanding of each principle and therefore, their ability to practice it and appreciate it. Also, children may plan special programs, according to their preference in programs, performances, etc. The zawadi were traditionally given to the children on the last day of Kwanzaa, January 1, but in the final analysis, latitude is left for the parents to decide the actual day of the Kwanzaa week for gift-giving.

Each day can also have different activities for adults as well as children. Adults usually plan night activities, especially since parents work during the day. So parents/adults may plan different cultural/heritage-building activities for these days. Activities that bring us closer together and increase the close bonds we should already have are encouraged, for Kwanzaa above all, is to reinforce the bonds between us as a people and give us a special opportunity to enjoy the celebration of ourselves and our history.

The Participation of Children

Kwanzaa is a holiday with meaning and roles for all ages, especially children. Whatever the level of comprehension and capacity for participation, children must be allowed and encouraged to participate in Kwanzaa as fully as they are able. To reduce the children to mere recipients of gifts is to duplicate one of the most negative aspects of some Christmas celebrations. Kwanzaa, by its very purpose and principles, requires the full active participation of children. The principles are especially for them, for they are our future. Therefore, unless they learn and absorb these principles, the hope we have in them is futile or at best, on shaky foundations.

Children can participate in various ways. First, they should and can learn, recite and explain the Principles each day at meal times or in a special setting for it. Secondly, they can light the mishumaa for each day and explain each principle. Thirdly, children can help make Kwanzaa cards and other Kwanzaa items, and they can also help make and put up Kwanzaa decorations. This assistance would, in fact, be practice and encouragement of the sixth principle, Kuumba. Children are very creative at early ages and should be encouraged to maintain and develop such a capacity and interest. And Kwanzaa provides an ideal instructive and inspirational context for this.

Fourthly, children can help prepare special foods and the setting for Kwanzaa meals. They need not be given the responsibility for an entire meal, but they should be given a small but meaningful project which would in turn enhance the meaning and enjoyment of Kwanzaa for them. Finally, children can and should be encouraged to make dramatic, musical and dance presentations in celebration of Kwanzaa at home, school or in the context of their organization. These are just a few main ways children can and should be encouraged to participate. There are countless others and with a little Kuumba adults can discover and encourage them.

Conclusion

As mentioned above, it is only appropriate that we end with the tamshi la tutaonana. For it is a clear and concise statement of values and vision we must cherish and maintain if we are to liberate ourselves and reshape reality in our own image and according to own needs and interests.

TAMSHI LA TUTAONANA
(The Farewell Statement)

Strive for discipline, dedication and achievement in all you do. Dare struggle and sacrifice and gain the strength that comes from this. Build where you are and dare leave a legacy that will last as long as the sun shines and the water flows. Practice daily Umoja, Kujichagulia, Ujima, Ujamaa, Nia, Kuumba and Imani. And may the wisdom of the ancestors always walk with us. May the year's end meet us laughing and stronger. May our children honor us by following our example in love and struggle. And at the end of next year, may we sit again together, in larger numbers, with greater achievement and closer to liberation and a higher level of human life.

HARAMBEE!   **HARAMBEE!**   **HARAMBEE!**

HARAMBEE!   **HARAMBEE!**   **HARAMBEE!**

HARAMBEE!

Chapter 6

FUNDAMENTAL QUESTIONS ABOUT KWANZAA:
An Interview

Editor's note: Below are some of the most frequently asked questions about Kwanzaa which we put to the creator of Kwanzaa, Dr. Maulana Karenga. The answers to them offer not only a concise view of the origin and meaning of Kwanzaa but also the dynamic context in which it evolved and continues to develop.

1.   Why was Kwanzaa created?

Kwanzaa was created:

To reaffirm the communitarian vision and values of African culture and to contribute to its restoration among African peoples in the Diaspora, beginning with Africans in America and expanding to include the world African community.

• To introduce and reinforce the Nguzo Saba, the Seven Principles and through this, introduce and reaffirm communitarian values and practices which strengthen and celebrate family, community and culture. These seven communitarian African values are: Umoja (Unity), Kujichagulia (Self-Determination), Ujima (Collective Work and Responsibility), Ujamaa (Cooperative Economics), Nia (Purpose), Kuumba (Creativity), and Imani (Faith) (See also definition of principles on page 5-6).

- To serve as a regular communal celebration which reaffirmed and reinforced the bonds between us as a people in the U.S., in the Diaspora and on the African continent, in a word, as a world African community. It was designed to unite and to strengthen African communities.

- As an act of cultural self-determination, as a self-conscious statement of our own unique cultural truth as an African people. That is to say, it is an important way and expression of being African in a multicultural context.

2.   Where does the word "Kwanzaa" come from?

The word "Kwanzaa" comes from the phrase, "matunda ya kwanza" which means "first-fruits." Kwanzaa's extra "a" evolved as a result of a particular history of the Organization Us. It was done as an expression of African values in order to inspire the creativity of our children. In the early days of Us, there were only seven children and each wanted to represent a letter of Kwanzaa. Since kwanza (first) has only six letters, we added an extra "a" to make it seven, thus creating "Kwanzaa."

3.   Why is Kwanzaa a seven-day holiday?

Kwanzaa is a seven-day holiday for two reasons:

*   In terms of authenticity, Kwanzaa is modeled on first-fruits celebrations in ancient Africa, especially on Southern African first-fruits celebrations like *Umkhosi* of Zululand which has seven days.

*   The central reason for Kwanzaa's being seven days is to stress the Nguzo Saba and through this introduce and reaffirm communitarian values and practices which strengthen and celebrate family, community, and culture.

4.   Why has Kwanzaa grown among African people?

Kwanzaa grows among African people because:

*   It speaks to our need and appreciation for its cultural vision and life-affirming values, values which celebrate and reinforce family, community, and culture.

*   It represents an important way Africans speak our own special cultural truth in a multicultural world.

*   It reaffirms the most ancient tradition in the world, the African tradition, which lays claim

to the first religious, ethical and scientific texts, and the introduction of the basic disciplines of human knowledge in the Nile Valley.

- It reinforces our rootedness in our own culture in a rich and meaningful way.

- It brings us together from all countries, all religious traditions, all classes, all ages and generations, and all political persuasions on the common ground of our Africanness in all its historical and current diversity and unity.

5.   **Can people who are not of African descent participate in Kwanzaa activities?**

Kwanzaa is clearly an African holiday created for African peoples. But other people can and do celebrate it, just like other people participate in Cinco de Mayo besides Mexicans; Chinese New Year besides Chinese; Native American pow wows besides Native Americans.

The question is, under what circumstances? There are both communal and public celebrations. One can properly hold a communal celebration dedicated essentially to community persons. But in a public context, say public school or college, we can properly have public celebrations which include others. How this is done depends on particular circumstances. But in any case, particular people should always be in control of and conduct their own celebrations. Audience attendance is one thing; conducting a ritual is another.

Any particular message that is good for a particular people, if it is human in its content and ethical in its grounding, speaks not just to that people, it speaks to the world.

The principles of Kwanzaa and the message of Kwanzaa has a universal message for all people of good will. It is rooted in African culture, and we speak as Africans speak, not just to ourselves, but to the world. This continues our tradition of making our own unique contribution to the forward flow of human history.

6.   **How is Kwanzaa related to our struggle to achieve social justice and build a better world?**

Kwanzaa organizes people, gives them a chance to ingather, and to reinforce the bonds between them, and to focus on positive cultural values and practice. And in reinforcing the bonds between us and reaffirming us in the best of our values, we are strengthened in our struggle for a morally grounded and empowered community, a just and good society and a world of peace and freedom.

Kwanzaa helps us to focus on the collective aspect of what we are about as a people with its focus on ingathering of the people, special reverence for the Creator and creation, commemoration of the past, recommitment to our highest values, and celebration of the good in life.

Kwanzaa was created out of the philosophy of Kawaida, which is a cultural nationalist philosophy that argues that the key challenge in Black people's life is the challenge of culture, and that what Africans must do is to discover and bring forth the best of their culture, both ancient and current, and use it as a foundation to bring into being models of human excellence and possibilities to enrich and expand our lives.

It was created in 1966 in the midst of our struggles for liberation and was part of our organization Us' efforts to create, recreate and circulate African culture as an aid to building community, enriching Black consciousness, and reaffirming the value of cultural grounding for life and struggle.

7.   How does Kwanzaa improve self-esteem?

Kwanzaa is not about self-esteem. Kwanzaa is about rootedness in your culture, knowledge of our culture and encouragement to act and create in such a way that *self-respect* will come of itself.

When you focus just on self-esteem you focus on individual orientation and that is against African values. We must focus on standing worthy before our people. Because we live in an individualistic society, people put such emphasis on self-gratification and self-indulgence they do not see that there is a collective aspect to what we are about as a people. The need is to root oneself in one's culture, extract its models of excellence and possibility and emulate them in our ongoing efforts to be the best of what it means to be African and human.

8.   Is Kwanzaa becoming commercialized?

We must make a distinction here between normal Ujamaa or the cooperative economic practice of artists and vendors to provide Kwanzaa materials and the corporate world's move to penetrate and dominate the community Kwanzaa market.

Operating with the primary purpose of making profits, corporate strategy consists of capitalizing on the African community's expanding practice of Kwanzaa and the accompanying expanding need for symbols and other items essential and related to the practice. To do this, these corporations will offer the standard enticements of convenience, variety, self-focus and self indulgence, ethnic imagery and other stimulants to cultivate and expand the consumer mind-set.

Moreover, they will camouflage their purely commercial interest in Kwanzaa by borrowing the language and symbols of the holiday itself to redefine it along commercial lines. Manipulating the language and symbols of Kwanzaa, they will seek not only to sell corporation-generated Kwanzaa items, but also to introduce a full range of corporate products as necessary for the practice of Kwanzaa. Thus, they will attempt not only to penetrate and dominate the Kwanzaa market, taking it from small-scale African American producers and vendors, but also redefine both the meaning and focus of Kwanzaa, making it another holiday of maximum and compelling shopping if we allow it.

9.   How do people resist the commercialization of Kwanzaa?

The challenge, for the African American community as well as African communities everywhere is to resist the corporate commercialization of Kwanzaa; to reaffirm and hold to the essential meaning of Kwanzaa and refuse to cooperate with the corporate drive to dominate and redefine it and make it simply another holiday to maximize sales.

By upholding the philosophy and principles of Kwanzaa, Black people can and do pose a strong wall against the waves of commercialization which affect all holidays in this market culture which is essentially a culture of sales and consumption. For Kwanzaa is above all a cultural practice not a commercial one and external or internal attempts to redefine Kwanzaa in commercial terms are not defining Kwanzaa, but rather their commercial interest in it.

The wall of resistance to commercialization, then, is the people themselves and their conscientious and consistent focus on the vision of Kwanzaa and the practice of its values. Certainly, the central values of Kwanzaa are the Nguzo Saba, the Seven Principles: Umoja (Unity); Kujichagulia (Self-Determination); Ujima (Collective Work and Responsibility); Ujamaa (Cooperative Economics); Nia (Purpose); Kuumba (Creativity); and Imani (Faith). And the conscientious and consistent practice of these values provide an effective defense against the waves of commercialism which are defining features of a market culture.

• The principles and practice of Umoja and Ujima require that celebrants stand in unity and assume collective responsibility for resistance to the commercialization and thus adulteration of Kwanzaa.

• Nia, the central purpose of community building as a collective vocation requires the defense of African culture and its highest values as expressed in Kwanzaa.

• Kujichagulia demands a practice of self-determination in both the cultural and economic sense. It stresses the moral obligation of Africans to define themselves, speak for themselves, build for themselves, and make their own unique contribution to the forward flow of human history. Thus this principle prohibits collaboration in one's own oppression, the allowance of others to define African people or culture and turning to others for

Kwanzaa items which the community itself has conceived of and has historically and rightfully made.

- Kuumba insists on community creativity, specifically during Kwanzaa and especially providing its own symbols.

- Ujamaa (cooperative economics) specifically requires control, not only of the economics of Kwanzaa, but also the very economy of the Black community in a mutually-beneficial process of shared work and shared wealth. No serious celebrants of Kwanzaa can support a corporate control of the economy of the Black community or the economics of Kwanzaa. Nor can they in good conscience drive small-scale community artists, producers, and vendors out of business by buying corporate products and aiding their penetration and domination of the Kwanzaa market.

- Imani (faith) stresses the spiritual and ethical resistance to market values which undermine and distort the sacred and significant. It is an ancient African teaching of Egypt which says that through our culture and its spirituality and ethics, we are given that which endures in the midst of that which is overthrown, that which is permanent in the midst of that which passes away. Thus, the vision and values of Kwanzaa are in opposition to the commercialism of a market culture, upholds the sacred and significant and poses principles of African family, community and culture which enrich and expand human life rather than reduce it to a market calculation of the opportunity and promise of sales. In this way, Kwanzaa stands as an excellent representative of that which endures in the midst of that which is over-thrown and that which is permanent in the midst of that which passes away.

10.   Can people celebrate Kwanzaa and Christmas? Is Kwanzaa an alternative to Christmas?

Kwanzaa was not created to give people an alternative to their own religion or religious holiday. And it is not an alternative to people's religion or faith but a common ground of African culture.

One of the most important and meaningful ways to see and approach Kwanzaa is as a self-conscious cultural choice. Some celebrants see Kwanzaa as an alternative to the sentiments and practices of other holidays which stress the commercial or faddists or lack an African character or aspect. But they realize this is not Kwanzaa's true function or meaning. For Kwanzaa is not a reaction or substitute for anything. In fact, it offers a clear and self-conscious option, opportunity and chance to make a proactive choice, a self-affirming and positive choice as distinct from a reactive one.

Likewise, Kwanzaa is a cultural choice as distinct from a religious one. This point is important because when the question arises as to the relation between choosing Kwanzaa or/and Christmas, this distinction is not always made. This failure to make this distinction causes confusion, for it appears to suggest one must give up one's religion to practice one's culture. Whereas this might be true in other cases, it is not so in this case. For here, one can and should make a distinction between one's specific religion and one's general culture in which that religion is practiced. On one hand, Christmas is a religious holiday for Christians, but it is also a cultural holiday for Europeans. Thus, one can accept and revere the religious message and meaning but reject its European cultural accretions of Santa Claus, reindeer, mistletoe, frantic shopping, alienated gift-giving, etc.

This point can be made by citing two of the most frequent reasons Christian celebrants of Kwanzaa give for turning to Kwanzaa. The first reason is that it provides them with cultural grounding and reaffirmation as African Americans. The other reason is that it gives them a spiritual alternative to the commercialization of Christmas and the resultant move away from its original spiritual values and message. Here it is of value to note that there is a real and important difference between spirituality as a general appreciation for and commitment to the transcendent, and religion which suggests formal structures and doctrines. Kwanzaa is not a religious holiday, but a cultural one with an inherent spiritual quality as with all major African celebrations.

This inherent spiritual quality is respect for the Transcendent, the Sacred, the Good, the Right. Thus, Africans of all faiths can and do celebrate Kwanzaa, i.e., Muslims, Christians, Black Hebrews, Jews, Buddhists, Bahai and Hindus as well as those who follow the ancient traditions of Maat, Yoruba, Ashanti, Dogon, etc. For what Kwanzaa offers is not an alternative to their religion or faith but *a common ground of African culture* which they all share and cherish. It is this common ground of culture on which they all meet, find ancient and enduring meaning and by which they are thus reaffirmed and reinforced.

11. **In some cases people have added things to their celebration of Kwanzaa which seem to differ from its original vision and value. How should those who want to maintain the original vision and values and at the same time allow for diversity within the holiday respond to this?**

The original vision and values of Kwanzaa must be maintained and nothing should be advocated or practiced which violates the original spirit, basic purpose and essential concepts which informed the creation and practice of Kwanzaa. However, two principles of Kwanzaa encourage creativity, diversity and flexibility within this general rule. These are Kuumba (creativity) and Kujichagulia (self-determination). So not only do we expect diversity of approaches as is true in any other holiday, but again as in other holidays, this diversity must be within a framework that strengthens the holiday not undermine it. The need is for established practices and standards which constitute the identity and essence of the holiday. Otherwise, the holiday does not exist and is no more than individual approaches with no meaning except to the persons doing them. Creativity calls for new and beautiful ways of celebrating the holiday not producing things and engaging in practices which destroy or diminish its value and meaning to us as a people. Self-determination calls for personal and collective expression which celebrate the holiday in unique ways not in self-indulgent ways which undermine the common ground of views and values which give the holiday its identity, meaning and value.

12.   Kwanzaa stresses value orientation. Why is this so important?

Values and value orientation are important, as Kawaida philosophy teaches, because values are categories of commitment, priorities and excellence which indicate and enhance human possibilities. Kwanzaa puts forth seven key values, the Nguzo Saba (The Seven Principles) which offer standards of excellence and models of possibilities and which aid in building and reinforcing family, community and culture: Umoja, Kujichagulia, Ujima, Ujamaa, Nia, Kuumba, Imani.

At the same time Kwanzaa reinforces associated values of truth, justice, propriety, harmony, balance, reciprocity and order. In a word, it reminds us to hold to our ancient traditions as a people who are spiritually grounded, who respect our ancestors and elders, cherish and challenge our children, care for the vulnerable, relate rightfully to the environment and always seek and embrace the Good.

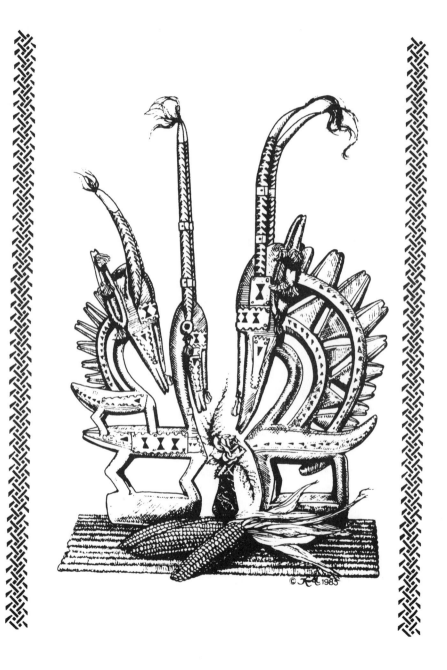

Chapter 7

SWAHILI TERMINOLOGY

Introduction

We chose Swahili as the most appropriate cultural language in 1965 for African Americans for three basic reasons. First, it is "non-ethnic" or "non-tribal" and thus, shows no ethnic or so-called "tribal" preference. Choice of any other African language would in fact show this. Secondly, we chose it because, being non-ethnic, it is Pan-African in character and so are we, African Americans, who claim all the people and the whole continent of Africa rather than one people or place on the continent.

Finally, we chose Swahili as a matter of self-determination according to our own needs and understanding and reject attempts to identify it with enslavement in order to discredit it. First, not only is that false, but if we are to reject speaking all languages associated with enslavement, by the same logic, we would have to begin by rejecting English and all other European languages. Secondly, the African people of Burundi, the Comoro Islands, Congo Republic, Kenya, Malagasy Republic, Malawi, Mozambique, Rwanda, Somali Republic, Tanzania, Zaire, and Zambia find it of value and valid.

Swahili pronunciation is extremely easy. The vowels are pronounced like those of Spanish and the consonants, with only a few exceptions, like those of English. The vowels are as follows: a = ah as in father; e = a as in day; i = ee as in free; o = o as in go; u = oo as in too. The accent is almost always on the penultimate syllable, i.e., next to the last syllable, except for a few words borrowed from Arabic which are irrelevant here.

Swahili Words Used During Kwanzaa (Swahili-English)

Swahili	English
asante	thank you
bendera	flag(s)
Habari gani?	What news?
harambee	let's all pull together
imani	faith
karamu	feast(s)
kikombe (sg.), vikombe (pl.)	cup(s)
kinara (sg.), vinara (pl.)	candle holder(s)
kujichagulia	self-determination
kuumba	creativity
Kwanzaa yenu iwe na heri	Happy Kwanzaa
mkeka (sg.), mikeka (pl.)	mat(s)
mshumaa(sg.), mishumaa (pl.)	candle(s)
mzee (sg.), wazee (pl.)	elder(s)

nguzo	principle(s)
nia	purpose
saba	seven
suke (sg.), masuke (pl.) muhindi (sg. & pl.)	ear(s) of corn
tafadhali	please
tambiko (sg.), matambiko (pl.)	libation(s)
tamshi (sg.), matamshi (pl.)	statement(s)
tunda (sg.), matunda (pl.)	fruit(s)
tutaonana	We will see each other.
ujamaa	cooperative economics
ujima	collective work and responsibility
umoja	unity
zao (sg.), mazao (pl.)	crop(s)
zawadi	gift(s)

Swahili Words Used During Kwanzaa (English-Swahili)

English	Swahili
candle holder(s)	kinara (sg.), vinara (pl.)
candle(s)	mshumaa (sg.), mishumaa (pl.)
collective work and responsibility	ujima
cooperative economics	ujamaa
creativity	kuumba
crop(s)	zao (sg.), mazao (pl.)
cup(s)	kikombe (sg.), vikombe (pl.)
ear(s) of corn	suke (sg.), masuke (pl.), muhindi (sg. & pl.)
elder(s)	mzee (sg.), wazee (pl.)
faith	imani
feast(s)	karamu

flag(s)	bendera
fruit(s)	tunda (sg.), matunda (pl.)
gift(s)	zawadi
Happy Kwanzaa	Kwanzaa yenu iwe na heri
let's all pull together	harambee
libation(s)	tambiko (sg.), matambiko (pl.)
mat(s)	mkeka (sg.), mikeka (pl.)
please	tafadhali
principle(s)	nguzo
purpose	nia
self-determination	kujichagulia
seven	saba
statement(s)	tamshi (sg.), matamshi (pl.)
thank you	asante

English	Swahili
unity	umoja
We will see each other.	tutaonana
What news?	Habari gani?

NOTES

1. Diasporan is from Diaspora which means the dispersion or scattering of any people of common origin, culture, etc. Here it refers to "overseas" Africans, i.e., those not on the Continent.

2. Pan-Africanism - a philosophy and practice which affirms the common history, culture, interests and struggle of African people.

3. Kawaida - a philosophy of cultural and social change which defines culture as the necessary key concern and focus for the liberational and developmental activities of African people. See Maulana Karenga, *Kawaida Theory: A Communitarian African Philosophy*, Los Angeles: University of Sankore Press, 1997.

4. Swahili - a Pan-African language spoken in 13 African countries which was chosen by Us and many segments of the Black Movement as the definitive African American and Pan-African language because it is essentially non-ethnic and Pan-African. Also, many continental Africans advocate its use as the continental African language. Among its most notable advocates is Nobel Laureate in Literature, Wole Soyinka of Nigeria.

5. Kwanzaa's extra "a" evolved as a result of a particular history of the Organization Us. It was done as an expression of African values in order to accommodate the wishes and inspire the creativity of our children. At the very beginning of Us, the seven children in the organization wanted to put on a program in which each of them

represented and explained a letter of Kwanzaa. Since kwanza (first) has only six letters, we added an extra "a" to make it seven, thus creating *Kwanzaa*. It did not essentially change the pronunciation and most important, it demonstrated our principle of *priority of the person in the context of community*. It also was an indication of the humanistic and value stress in Kwanzaa.

6.   J. Omosade Awolalu, *Yoruba Beliefs and Sacrificial Rites*, London: Longman, 1979, pp. 143ff.

7.   D.G. Coursey, "The New Yam Festival Among the Ewe," *Ghana Notes and Queries*, 10 (December) 1986.

8.   J.B. Danquah, *Gold Coast: Akan Laws and Customs and the Abuakwa Constitution*, London: George Rutledge and Sons, Ltd., 1928, p. 129.

9.   W.C. Willoughby, *The Soul of the Bantu*, Garden City, NY: Doubleday, Doran & Co., 1928, pp. 235, 237; Max Gluckman, "Social Aspects of First-Fruits Celebrations and the South Eastern Bantu," *Africa*, 11, 1 (January, 1938) p. 25; O.F. Raum "The Interpretation of the Nguni First-Fruits Ceremony," *Paideuma*, Vol. 13, 1967.

10.   Reconstructed from fragments in Henri Junod, *The Life of a South African Tribe*, New York: University Books, 1966, Vol. 1, p. 401.

11.   Awolalu, op. cit., p. 145.

12. Reconstructed from fragments in Peter Sarpong, *The Sacred Stools of the Akan*, Accra-Tema: Ghana Publishing Company, 1971, pp. 66ff.

13. Henri Frankfort, *Kingship and the Gods*, Chicago: University of Chicago Press, 1948, pp. 188ff.

14. E.H. Mends, "Ritual in the Social Life of Ghanaian Society," in J.M. Assimeng (ed.), *Traditional Life, Culture and Literature in Ghana*, New York: Cinch Magazine Limited, 1976 p. 8.

15. Libation - a liquid poured as an offering in worship or veneration.

16. Maulana Karenga, *Selections From the Husia: Sacred Wisdom of Ancient Egypt*, Los Angeles: University of Sankore Press, 1984, p. 111

17. Nguzo Saba (The Seven Principles); see pp. 35ff.

18. Awolalu, op. cit., p. 149.

19. Karenga, *Kwanzaa: Origin, Concepts, Practice*, Los Angeles: Kawaida Publications, 1977, p. 18.

20. Karenga, op. cit., 1997.

21. Sekou Toure, *Toward Full Re-Africanization*, Paris Presence Africane, 1959.

22.   Karenga, op. cit., 1984, p. 39ff.

23.   Ibid., pp. 64, 41, 67.

24.   Francis Deng, *The Dinka of the Sudan*, New York: Holt, Rhinehart & Winston, 1972, pp. 13ff.

25.   Ibid., p. 14.

26.   W.E.B. DuBois, *W.E.B. DuBois: Writings*, New York: Library of America, 1986, p. 861.

27.   Ifeanyi Menkiti, "Person and Community in African Traditional Thought" in Richard Wright (ed.), *African Philosophy*, Washington, D.C.: University Press of America, Inc., 1984, p. 171.

28.   John Mbiti, African Religions and Philosophy, New York: Doubleday, p. 141.

29.   Menkiti, op. cit., p. 172.

30.   Karenga, op. cit., 1984, pp. 66, 32.

31.   John Mbiti, op. cit., p. 141.

32.   Kwame Gyekye, *An Essay on African Philosophical Thought - The Akan Conceptual Scheme*, New York: Cambridge University Press, 1987, p. 156.

33.   Ibid., p. 157.

34.   Ibid.

35.   Maulana Karenga, *Selections From the Husia: Sacred Wisdom of Ancient Egypt*, Los Angeles: University of Sankore Press, 1984, p. 111.

36.   Anna Julia Cooper, *A Voice From the South*, New York: Oxford University Press, 1988, p. 60.

37.   Elechi Amadi, *Ethics in Nigerian Culture*, Ibadan: Nigeria: Heinman Educational Books (Nigeria) Ltd., 1982, p. 54.

38.   Malcolm X, *Malcolm X Speaks*, New York: Merit Publishers, 1965, p. 4ff.

39.   Irene Gendzier, *Frantz Fanon, A Critical Study*, New York: Pantheon Books, 1973, p. 3.

40.   Maulana Karenga, "Black Studies and the Problematic of Paradigm, *Journal of Black Studies*," 18, 4 (June) 1988, p. 404.   See also Molefi Asante, *The Afro-Centric Idea*, Philadelphia: Temple University Press, 1987.

41.   J.D. and E.J. Krige, "The Lovedu of the Transvaal," In Darryl Forde (ed.), *African Worlds: Studies in the Cosmological Ideals and Social Values of African Peoples*, New York: Oxford University Press, 1965, pp. 76ff.

42. Ibid., p. 77.

43. Maulana Karenga, *Kawaida Theory: An Introductory Outline,* Los Angeles: University of Sankore Press, 1984, pp. 62ff.

44. Julius Nyerere, *Freedom and Socialism/Uhuru na Ujamaa,* New York: Oxford University Press, 1969, p. 316.

45. Ibid., p. 318.

46. Karenga, op. cit., 1984, p.54.

47. Ibid., p. 47.

48. Ibid., p. 111.

49. National Education Association, *The Legacy of Mary McLeod Bethune,* Washington, D.C.: NEA, 1974, p. 18.

50. Frantz Fanon, *The Wretched of the Earth,* New York: Grove Press, 1968, p. 167.

51. Maulana Karenga, "Restoration of the Husia: Revising a Sacred Legacy" in Maulana Karenga and Jacob Carruthers (eds.), *Kemet and the African Worldview,* Los Angeles: University of Sankore Press, 1986, p. 97.

52. NEA, op. cit., p. 17.

53.   Formerly the words *kibunzi* and *vibunzi* were colloquially used for ear of corn and ears of corn respectively. But technically this is not correct. Kibunzi is technically cob of corn or corn cob. And suke la muhindi or masuke ya muhindi means ear of corn or ears of corn respectively. Suke literally means the seed-bearing head or ear of various grain plants, i.e., rice, millet, corn, but corn or another plant is referred to, it is understood that suke refers to it specifically.

The decision was made to return to the generic word for corn in the Kwanzaa setting, because this was originally what was used in the early celebrations and thus, such a return would restore common terminology for corn. Suke (masuke) is given simply for those who wish to say precisely ear of corn. But muhindi can be used to refer to corn in general and to the ears of corn themselves.

54.   Marcel Griaule, *Conversations with Ogotemmeli*, New York: Oxford University Press, 1980, p. 138.

55.   Karenga, op. cit., 1984, p. 109.

56.   Ibid., p. 53.

57.   Imhotepian means essentially multidimensional, multi-talented. It is derived from the name Imhotep (c. 2700 BCE, Old Kingdom), an ancient Egyptian who was an architect (built the first pyramid), engineer, physician (worshiped as the god of medicine by the Greeks), prime minister, priest, author and philosopher. In a Eurocentric

conceptualization, such a man would be called a Renaissance man.

58. A talasimu is the symbol of the Organization Us which is at the same time a heritage symbol. It is an African face framed by a triangle and which has, as eyes and nose, three pyramids symbolic of African traditional greatness, a star which is Garvey's star of unity and three neck-rings symbolic of the three ends of Black Power -- self-determination, self-respect and self-defense.

59. Quoted in Maulana Karenga, *Maat, The Moral Ideal in Ancient Egypt: A Study in Classical African Ethics.* Unpublished dissertation, University of Southern California, 1994, p.748.

60. J.B. Danquah, op. cit., p. 127.

INDEX